SHARING SACRED SPACE

MONASTIC INTERRELIGIOUS DIALOGUE SERIES

Sharing Sacred Space

Interreligious Dialogue as Spiritual Encounter

Benoît Standaert

Translated by William Skudlarek

LITURGICAL PRESS
Collegeville, Minnesota

www.litpress.org

Cover design by David Manahan, OSB

© 2003, Uitgeverij Lannoo nv. for the original edition. Original title: *De Jezusruimte*. www.lannoo.com

1	2	3	4	5	6	7	8

Library of Congress Cataloging-in-Publication Data

Standaert, Benoît.
    [Jezusruimte. English]
    Sharing sacred space : interreligious dialogue as spiritual encounter / Benoît Standaert ; translated by William Skudlarek.
        p.   cm.
    ISBN 978-0-8146-3280-2
    1. Christianity and other religions.   2. Jesus Christ—Person and offices.   3. Spirituality.   4. Spiritual life.   5. Sacred space.   I. Title.
BR127.S774513   2009
261.2—dc22

                                        2009019125

Contents

Introduction
to the English Edition

I wish to express my thanks to Saint John's Abbey and to Liturgical Press for having asked Fr. William Skudlarek to undertake this translation. With the exception of a few pages of my work that have appeared in India, this is the first time anything I have written has been published in English. I am most grateful to them for making this debut possible.

What appears here is only the third and last part of my book, *L'Espace Jésus*. It originally appeared in Dutch with the title *De Jezusruimte* (Lannoo, 2000), then in Italian (Áncora, 2004), and two years later in French (Lessius, 2006). All authors feel a certain loving protectiveness for the works they have brought to light, and for this reason I regret that only a part of what I conceived of as a whole is being published in English. At the same time, the final section of my book is what is most original and innovative, and I would like to think that after becoming familiar with the third and last part, some readers might be interested in exploring the rest of this larger work.

I welcome this edition with gratitude and with the hope that these pages may inspire all who engage in interreligious dialogue to advance the unity of the human family. Together may we make our way to what lies beyond our most noble efforts: the peace that is one of the names of God in so many of the world's religious traditions.

Spiritual Space

In writing *L'Espace Jésus* I set out to elaborate a new way of speaking about Christian faith before undertaking the challenge of entering into dialogue with other religions. A central intuition guided my efforts. Any encounter with the great religions of the world is doomed to fail if its starting point is dogma as formulated and transmitted in a given culture, or if it is based on some historical expressions, which are also culturally conditioned. If we want to provide a level playing field for all the participants, we have to come up with some other approach. In order to make it possible for us to meet one another as equals, I have made use of the category of "spiritual space."[1]

Each great religious tradition exists in a specific spiritual space. For the Christian it is "Jesus space" or "Christ space." In like manner, there is a specific spiritual space for the Jewish tradition, with its distinctive periods and concerns—for example, the rabbinic period with the Talmud, the Kabbalistic period, the Hassidic movement. It is also possible to refer to a Qurʾanic space and a Buddhist space. We can also speak of spiritual space with regard to agnostics, for they can be open to and even eager for an encounter with a religious space like that of Jesus.

The Phenomenon and Meaning of "Jesus Space"

Whoever calls on the name of Jesus with faith enters into a unique spiritual space. This space obviously has to do with a historical individual who lived some twenty centuries ago, but

---

[1] The category of "spiritual space" can be found quite often in contemporary works. I first came across it in the writings of the philosopher Louis Lavelle, especially in his book *L'erreur de Narcisse* (1939), the last chapter of which is entitled "Spiritual Space." Maurice Bellet is another contemporary intellectual who often thinks in terms of space. In a recent book of his I found the same expression I am using here: "Jesus space."

it includes much more than that. The space has also been shaped by the authoritative dogmatic formulas that issued from the ecumenical councils of the fourth and fifth centuries. At the same time, it is a vibrant, living space that surpasses all definitions, even dogmatic ones.

By the concept of "space," I mean a *category* that includes the Jesus whom we can access through critical historical research, as well as the Christ who is professed by faith and defined in dogma. The category of "Jesus space" transcends the limits proper to historical discourse as well as those proper to dogmatic formulations. Jesus means much more to the Christian believer than these two approaches can ever tell us about him.

The category of "space" is similar to what Teilhard de Chardin was referring to when he spoke of a divine milieu. From a phenomenological point of view, it suggests a spiritual semantic field that can be expressed in concrete terms. Hermeneutically speaking, however, the meaning of "space" is intentionally spiritual. The "space" field is tantamount to a paradoxical "circle," one "whose center is everywhere and whose circumference is nowhere." The freedom that "Jesus space" brings with it cannot be kept in check. It is expressed in all sorts of creative ways, but can only be known from the inside. This does not in any way imply that there is arbitrariness about the all-encompassing openness of this space. There are limits to how it is to be understood and what it includes. If you are outside this space, then it simply does not exist for you. On the other hand, no matter how much you draw on it, it will never be exhausted. A simple gesture, like making the sign of the cross or gazing upon an icon, may be all it takes to make this space present within you once again. Very little is required. However, even the most solemn celebrations—those of Easter and Pentecost, for example—cannot deplete the fullness of "Jesus space."

In this particular treatment of the category of spiritual space, I have made use of both a phenomenological and a hermeneutical/spiritual approach, referring to dogmatic definitions and historical criticism only insofar as they confirm or raise questions about my interpretation.

From a strictly cognitive point of view, I believe it is necessary to be clear about something right at the beginning. Reality is one. However, our knowledge of it is limited. The process of knowing can be described in terms of circles that are intertwined and at the same time transcend one other. As I see it, what is most physical, definite, and historical—what can be materially "proven"—makes up the first circle. It, in turn, opens up to the circle of a wider and more elevated psychic and cultural reality, with its types and "antitypes." This is the circle of knowledge and intuition, and it abounds in connotations and connections of every sort. It is much more flexible than the "hard" first circle, which, because it is rooted in history, is what it is and nothing else.

A third circle issues from the second and extends even further than the first two. This is the realm of the truly spiritual. In contrast to the materiality of the first circle, what is specific to this third circle is its transcendence. Paradox makes its appearance here: gain is loss; you save your life by giving it up; the one who is humbled will be exalted; the poor are declared rich; the satisfied are sent away empty-handed; the captive sings and shouts for joy with a freedom that cannot be held in check. Here we understand what Jesus meant when he said, "The wind blows where it chooses, and you hear the sound of it, but you do not know where it comes from or where it goes." Jesus was speaking about a current of air, but at the same time he was pointing to another, supremely free reality, one that in Hebrew and Greek is expressed by the same word: Spirit. Lest anyone not understand what reality he was speaking of, Jesus added, "So it is with everyone who is born of the Spirit" (John 3:8).

There is a final circle that far surpasses and contains all the others: the circle of the divine. This is not simply a fourth circle alongside the other three. I truly believe that this circle not only includes the other three but penetrates them and supports them from within.

In our consideration of "Jesus space," we need to be aware of this fourfold characteristic of reality. The art of understanding, like the art of living, consists in augmenting the first circle by the second, which in turn, ought, as far as possible, to be filled by the third. As we do this we are constantly more aware that the divine penetrates and renews everything to the degree that we give our consent to it. Contrary to what has been accepted as true for centuries, the art of living does not consist in abandoning the first circle for the second, and the second for the third. It is just the opposite. Life is lived at its fullest when the sublime shines forth in what is the most negligible and unassuming, when the unlimited is perceived in what is finite. Ever since the coming of Jesus our true task is not to "spiritualize" but constantly to "incarnate."

There are also consequences for purely historical research—insofar as it is possible to engage in a "purely historical" investigation. How beneficial this undertaking will be will only become apparent when we see where it leads us. Its richest and most abundant fruit will be found when we apply the category of spiritual space to interreligious dialogue and discover how much farther it will take us than a dialogue that only takes into account history or dogma. What is finally at stake is whether or not the religions of the world will be able to live in peace with one another in the future. For many today, interreligious peace is one of the main building blocks for the house of peace that our little blue planet is called to construct.

As noted above, very little—almost nothing, in fact—is required to open up the spiritual space in which the name of Jesus reigns supreme. But once it has been opened, this space must be nurtured so that we may continue to grow spiritually. Existence "in Christ," according to an expression dear to St. Paul, is one of continual growth (see 1 Thess 5:10; Phil 3:12-14, etc.). This space is nourished by study, prayer, and concrete acts of Christian charity—the "three pillars of the world,"[2] according to an ancient Jewish axiom that shaped the early Christian tradition. For a Christian, the art of living consists in dedicating oneself to the ongoing practice of study, prayer, and action in order to

---

[2] See the introductory chapter in Benoît Standaert, *Les trois colonnes du monde : Carnet de route pour le pèlerin du XXIe siècle* (Paris: Desclée, 1991). The sentence on the three columns of the world can be found in *Pirqé Avoth* 1, 2, where it is attributed to Simon the Just (about 200 BCE).

become more aware of the space in which Jesus shines forth, and then to live it more profoundly. Up to a certain point, we can say that anything can provide an entrance to this space because *everything speaks of Him* (see the hymn in Col 1:15-17).

The celebration of the Eucharist is at one and the same time the fullest expression of "Jesus space" and the supreme synthesis of study-prayer-action. The meaning of existence becomes especially clear to Christians when, gathered in community, they celebrate the presence of the risen One. Remembering his words and his actions, they are transformed in and by the Spirit during the course of symbolic acts carried out in faith. Prayer is nourished by the light of the word of God, and the Liturgy of the Eucharist, like every liturgical rite, serves to deepen and intensify the love of believers for one another and for everyone, including those outside the community of faith. Symbols are powerful, and each time we employ them, they continue their transforming work in us.

Jesus Space in the Scriptures

One of the privileged ways to allow ourselves to be filled by "Jesus space" is through the practice that monks refer to as *lectio divina*. The "sacred reading" of the Scriptures is done in such a way that we are drawn into the presence of God by God's coming to us. In other words, by reading, we allow ourselves to be "read" and approached by God, for God cannot be grasped or approached by our reading, no matter how it is done.

The whole of the Scriptures contains everything that can be found in "Jesus space." Each book speaks of Jesus, the Word made flesh, the sacrament of the encounter with God. The whole of the Scriptures speaks his name. "The entire Torah is God's Name," according to the teaching of the Jewish masters. All the letters of both the First and the New Testaments spell out the unique name of "Jesus" (*Yehoshua* in Hebrew), the Christ, the Son of God. The book of Psalms is a prime example. Those who learn to pray the Psalms in a Christian way are drawn by their internal movement of lamentation and praise to savor the saving power that is fully revealed in the event that is "Jesus."[3] Christian psalmody enlarges this unique "Jesus space." Jesus himself comes down to us in the words of the Psalms. He assumes these words, just as he completely assumed our human condition and made it the means by which he expressed the freedom of the Son, the abandonment of the Suffering Servant, and the fullness of his uninterrupted prayer in the Spirit. *In Him and through Him* is realized in us what the psalmist chanted long ago: "so that my soul may praise you and not be silent" (Ps 30:12).

While it is possible to discover "Jesus space" in the entire body of Sacred Scripture, there is a privileged place in which this space is eminently revealed: the twenty-seven texts that make up the New Testament. This early Christian collection of writings, which with a few exceptions dates from the first century, shows us how "Jesus space" originally took shape in the life of the first believers.

In the first part of *L'Espace Jésus*, I looked at 1 Thessalonians, Revelation, Hebrews, and Ephesians to demonstrate how different literary genres affect the way Jesus space is presented. I then turned to the four gospels as four literary worlds, each with its own view of and access to Jesus space. The New Testament offers a rich and varied assortment of the most ancient traditions about Jesus. Its richness still nourishes us today. Those who try too hard to construct a theological system out of these traditions will sooner or later betray an essential characteristic of the Christian tradition: its respect for pluralism.

Following this examination of the meaning of "Jesus space," I set off to discover Jesus himself. How was he perceived by the most ancient witnesses (Simon Peter, John, Paul, Mary), and how did he understand himself, his vocation, and his destiny? My research led me to do a more detailed analysis of the role of the Holy Spirit and of Jesus' own understanding of his divine sonship. I then concluded the first part with a brief portrait of Jesus in the context of his time.

---

[3] See Benoît Standaert, *La prière* (Québec: Anne Sigier, 2002), pp. 37–146, especially pp. 90–97.

The second part of the book centered on the originality of our Easter faith and on the language of the resurrection. This language is primarily theological: it tells us what *God* made clear to the disciples who bore witness to the resurrection. Following on the death of the one he had sent, God declared himself in solidarity with Jesus. He did not condemn but rather commended the life that had been offered up, thus going against the law that said, "Cursed [by God] is everyone who hangs on a tree" (Gal 3:13; see Deut 21:22). The first witnesses to the resurrection bore witness to God, to his word and his deed. Their witness reveals the prospect of life beyond the shameful crucifixion suffered by Jesus. We can therefore live as he lived, fully confident that even if we are violently attacked and die, we will fall into the hands of God, who always glorifies his true witnesses, his martyrs.

To conclude this reflection on the language of the resurrection, I invited the reader to the specific practice of the Jesus Prayer ("Lord Jesus Christ, Son of God, have mercy on me, a sinner") and to the contemplation of Rublev's icon of the Trinity, an icon shaped by the rhythm of this prayer of the heart. Thanks to such practices one's heart can rest in the spiritual space opened up by faith in the paschal mystery and "breathe Christ," as we are invited to do by St. Anthony, patriarch of monks in the East as well as the West (*Vita*, c. 20).

Strengthened by this new way of understanding who we are and by the invitation to enter fully into the spiritual space created by faith in the paschal mysteries, we are now prepared to encounter the other with humility. We have arrived, in other words, at the threshold of the third part of the book, the part that here appears in English translation.

Let us proceed on this way as pilgrims, that is to say, in a spirit of poverty, without any pretension of superiority. History shows us that for centuries we have despised others and even taught people that this was the proper way to act. What gives great cause for hope is the awareness that we are entering upon a new age in which dialogue, with its spirit of openness and its willingness for self-examination, draws us toward the realization of peace.

Those who are humble, no matter what their religion, always understand one another. "Blessed are the poor" was the powerful declaration of a teacher who accepted even the poverty of the cross. May this blessedness be the compass that is our constant guide.

A New Challenge

Thus, with Jesus space as our starting point, we can now set off to visit other spaces. On this small planet of ours, many different peoples have developed all-encompassing religious systems. As we come into contact with these world religions, we cannot avoid asking how they relate to one another. One of the most inspiring spiritual adventures of our time is to be found in the mutual encounter of Jews, Christians, Muslims, Buddhists, Hindus, Baha'is . . . . In each of these encounters a new challenge awaits us. Catholics have been strongly encouraged by the Second Vatican Council, especially in its declaration entitled *Nostra Aetate*, and by Popes Paul VI and John Paul II, to become engaged with these other religions.[4] An especially important step on this journey was taken at the world day of prayer for peace in Assisi on October 27, 1986.

Already Begun

Interreligious dialogue happens every day. It takes place on television, in the newspapers, in sports, and finally in our hearts.

---

[4] In his very first encyclical, *Ecclesiam Suam* (1964), Paul VI gave a central place to dialogue (called *colloquium* in the Latin original), and especially to interreligious dialogue. A recent book brings together all the official documents dealing with interreligious dialogue that appeared between 1963 and 1997. It runs to almost 1,000 pages! See Francesco Gioia, ed., *Interreligious Dialogue: The Official Teaching of the Catholic Church from the Second Vatican Council to John Paul II, 1963–2005* (Boston: Pauline Books and Media, 2006). From John Paul II alone there are 52 citations from his 13 encyclicals and 266 other statements dealing with interreligious dialogue.

Today everyone who is the least bit reflective will at some time or other deal with questions about the methods and disciplines of the spiritual life, experiment with meditation by using either an Eastern or a Western approach, come under the influence of a film that takes us into a Tibetan Buddhist monastery, or be amazed and overcome by the music of the Sufis. Dialogue is something we have all experienced, well before the experts told us what was possible and what was not, what was meaningful and what was irrelevant or even nonsense. Each of us is assembling building blocks for a new edifice because the culture we are a part of has shown us that it must be built.

I remember a television program on the German/French channel ARTE entitled *The Return of the Sacred*. For this lengthy documentary, the French cinematographer and philosopher Olivier Germain Thomas brought together a number of people who had never before been in touch with one another. Among them were Denys, a Tibetan lama who was French by birth, and Jean Vanier together with one of his communities for people with disabilities. We looked in on a healing session with a world-renowned Hindu woman, visited a therapeutic community in Switzerland, and listened to an interview with a spiritual father in a Western monastery. Thanks to the medium of television, this cinematographer was able to do something that surpassed what each of these spiritual masters was able to accomplish individually. Those who watched his program were compelled to take into account the whole of what they were seeing. They were being asked to make connections, to compare, and finally, to take the risk of coming up with a personal synthesis of all that is happening on the spiritual stage in our time.

Humbly and Resolutely

And yet, we have to recognize that we are dealing with something new. There are very few, if any, models we can follow. We feel our way through a field that is filled with riches but is also unknown. Some genuine pioneers have gone ahead of us and been reproached for betraying the faith.[5] Nonetheless, we have to make our way with a humble and open mind, without rigidly insisting that our position is the only right one. Going back is not an option. Our identity is not an outpost to be defended at all costs, nor a treasure we might lose, but the creative power of entering into relationship with others. The way will be long, but what gives us confidence is the conviction that what we have most in common is our future, which we hope will be one of peace.

The pages that follow are the fruit of extended and detailed reflection on the many ways in which we differ from one another. Actually meeting someone who is different from us allows us to experience a new world; subsequent study makes it possible to understand more deeply the discovery we have made. If we begin with study, then the experience of meeting someone who is from a different religion opens up new doors for study, offering nuances and particularities that cannot be found simply by reading books. What we ultimately aim for is an integration of the two poles of concrete experience and study.

I will undertake this exchange on three fronts: Jewish, Muslim, and Buddhist. Each relationship will be different, but it may happen that an engagement with one helps foster a relationship with the other. These dialogues, in other words, can be mutually beneficial. Each time I reflect on the meaning of a relationship with the other, I will do so by starting out from the spiritual space that is opened when the name of Jesus is called upon with faith. Finally, I will also consider whether or not Jesus space can also have meaning for the contemporary unbeliever, the agnostic.

---

[5] The Belgian Jesuit Jacques Dupuis, who lived in India for many years and then came to Rome in the 1990s to teach, had to leave his teaching post at the Gregorian University because of the criticism leveled against his works, even though they were grounded in serious and solid scholarship. See especially his major work *Toward a Christian Theology of Religious Pluralism* (Maryknoll, NY: Orbis Books, 1997).

The works I cite will provide an overview of the major themes of this study. For the most part, however, I want to reflect on what I have personally discovered as I walked the path of dialogue. I will keep to the valley and not attempt the kind of global overview or synthesis that is possible from the mountaintop. My only hope is that readers will recognize themselves in these pages and be enticed to take the risk of entering into this adventure of faith. At any rate, I am just a beginner. If I treat our relationship with Judaism more extensively, the reason is simple: Jesus the Jew is the one who binds us together—and who also separates us from one another. Can that paradox ultimately be understood apart from its historical expression over the centuries?

However we look at these matters, we journey together, with a past that sometimes separates us, but with a common future that already unites us. We are little more than poor pilgrims, marching to a common destination. We need to remember the biblical vision that is offered to us on several occasions in the First Testament: pilgrims set out from all the nations on the earth, marching toward the *visio pacis*, the place where God will establish peace. These pilgrims are not in a race, nor does anyone lord it over the others. On the contrary, as the prophet Zephaniah puts it, they march humbly, "shoulder to shoulder"—or more literally, "under one shoulder" (Zeph 3:9).[6] That prophetic vision has now become more real than ever as we learn to walk "shoulder to shoulder" with our brothers and sisters of other religions or of none.

Benoît Standaert
Bruges, September 26, 2008

---

[6] This passage is cited in *Nostra Aetate* (4). In the New Revised Standard Version it is translated "and serve him with one accord."

1

Jesus and Judaism

In Rocca di Garda, near the Garda Lake north of Verona where I have been staying for the past two weeks, there is hard work to be done: chopping, sawing, and pruning. Centuries-old cypresses and oaks, some dating back to the sixteenth or seventeenth century, have become tangled and have to be separated from one another or even chopped down completely. I admire the work of the woodsmen and tremble at the sound of those massive tree trunks as they fall to the ground from a height of thirty or forty feet. I am conscious of the fact that some of these noble trees have had to withstand the rigors of the changing seasons for more than three hundred years.

When I think again of Jesus, of Judaism, and of Christianity, made up essentially of Gentile converts, I am even more awestruck. Like the oak trees at Rocca di Garda, these two great traditions grew out of a single shoot and became entwined with one another. Of all the religions in the world, none is closer to us than Judaism. We have so much in common, and yet, even though we have never been all that distant from one another, we have grown up and become two very different bodies. Moreover, the Christian rejection of Judaism was so extreme that it gave rise to systematic persecutions and, in the twentieth century, to an attempt to wipe out Judaism as a people and as a religion. Just a little more than a half century ago six million Jews, one million of them children, met death in the furnaces and gas chambers of Europe. We still shudder, overcome with shame as we ask ourselves how this could have happened at the heart of a so-called "Christian" civilization. We look into the eyes of the other—the survivor, the escapee, the one who was not exterminated—and we stand condemned.

At the same time, we cannot be held prisoner by a shame that renders us mute. We have to go beyond the horror we feel and do all we can so that the forces of destruction will never again triumph over goodness, integrity, righteousness, truth, and justice. In spite of everything, we believe in that which is stronger than the impenetrable mystery of evil, and we continue to opt for goodness in spite of our pain and sorrow, our shame and guilt. Jesus himself, and the space of Jesus interiorized by our paschal faith, impels us to stand up, to move forward, and to encounter the other, all the while fully aware of what is demanded of us: "So when you are offering your gift at the altar, if you remember that your brother or sister has something against you, leave your gift there before the altar and go; first be reconciled to your brother or sister, and then come and offer your gift" (Matt 5:23-24). We need to be able to talk to one another again, but to begin with, we Christians need to be able to listen—just listen—to the other.

In the book of Job we read that three of his friends came to visit him. At first they simply sat next to him on the ash heap and kept silence. "They sat with him on the ground for seven days and seven nights, and no one spoke a word to him, for they saw that his suffering was very great" (Job 2:13). Even if these three "friends" ultimately proved unhelpful, it remains true, as Elie Wiesel comments, that what they did during that first week was commendable. They listened in order to learn how someone else sees things, understands the world, and tries to find some meaning in his suffering.

To learn how to accept one another without prejudice will not be easy. The main reason for this is the Shoah. It happened very recently—some seventy years ago—but only now, it seems, are we able to talk about it. But the Shoah is not the only reason. Both sides have worked out their theological systems without ever talking to one another. They have engaged in polemics, sometimes direct, sometimes veiled, and developed their defensive reflexes. Within each community, positions have been hammered into doctrines to protect against any possible seduction from the other camp. All this now goes under the name of orthodoxy within each of the two traditions. Where can we find a wise gardener or a woodsman with the skill and the authority to prune the wild shoots and create a *pardes*, a garden in which we can dwell with delight? Starting out from Jesus space, rather than from ready-made dogmatic formulas that come from a culture long gone, means that we will want to keep a careful distance from statements that are too weighty (they can serve us well *ad intra*, but *ad extra*?), all the while holding on to the central core of our faith in Christ Jesus.

At the very least, dialogue presupposes two conditions: confidence and accurate knowledge of others as they themselves want to be known. These two conditions are mutually supportive: the more accurate our knowledge of the other, the greater will be our confidence, and vice versa.

I write as a Christian and I direct what I have to say first of all to my brothers and sisters in Jesus Christ. But since I have received so much from the Jewish tradition over these past twenty years, I secretly hope that the reflections that follow will not only express my gratitude for the wisdom and insights I have received but may also serve to build a bridge between our two traditions. May the two find here whatever is needed to pass safely from one shore to the other.

To begin with, I will concentrate on Jesus the Jew and his Jewishness. Next I will look at how Judaism has developed over the centuries following the death of Jesus, and especially at how the arrival of many other messiahs has marked Jewish history down to the present day. Finally I will indicate three points of possible understanding between Jesus and Judaism as it has developed over the course of history.

The Question of the Jewishness of Jesus

About ten years ago the Jesuits at Heverlee, near Louvain/ Leuven, invited me to speak to them about Jesus. The questions they wanted me to address were, "To what degree is/was Jesus a Jew? What kind of Jew was he?"—questions I had actually been thinking about for months. I spontaneously started to question the questions—good Jewish methodology!—and even to object to them. Are these really questions? Are they good questions? Or are they only a way of stating the obvious? Do we have here new questions, the kind today's young people ask? Or are they simply the questions of someone who is curious, who would like to know a little more, would like to understand what the world was like in the first century, and nothing more? And finally, who is asking these questions, a Christian or a Jew?

There are, it seems, some people who are surprised by questions like these. Two examples. A priest friend of mine told me that he recently gave a lecture on the family tree of Jesus as it appears in the first chapter of Matthew. Someone in the hall responded by saying, "It never occurred to me that Jesus may have been a Jew. I'm going to have to think about that some more!" More recently someone told me about an ecumenical day that took place at Louvain-la-Neuve in the eighties. The title of the study day was "Jesus the Jew." An Orthodox theologian from one of the Eastern churches said openly, "For us Jesus is not a Jew. The Word was made flesh. The Incarnation means that he became a human being. The fact that he was a Jew is beside the point. It doesn't have to be dealt with."

These two reactions are sufficient to show that for us Christians, these questions raise a host of other questions. Why did it never occur to that gentleman that Jesus was a Jew? Why did the Eastern Orthodox theologian say, "For us, it's not even a question"? And why does this reaction surprise us—it surprises me, at least—to the point of causing annoyance and even shock? These may indeed be *new* questions, typical of the kind of questions that are asked in the last quarter of the twentieth century. When, in the seventies, Geza Vermes called his book *Jesus the*

Jew,[1] he wanted to do something more than state the obvious. When the German theologian Friedrich-Wilhelm Marquart wrote a new christological treatise and entitled it *The Christian Confession of Jesus the Jew: A Christology,*[2] his emphasis on the significance of the *Jewishness* of Jesus was what made his work unique. And when a collection of studies came out in 1991 with the noteworthy title *Jesus' Jewishness: Exploring the Place of Jesus within Early Judaism,*[3] it became obvious that questions concerning the Jewishness of Jesus were real, and that this was seen as something new.

Who asks these questions? Christians, apparently, though not *all* Christians. What about Jews? Some do, but for them the answer is obvious. There is no lack of books on Jesus written by Jews—beginning with Joseph Klausner, and then continuing with such authors as David Flusser, Schalom Ben-Chorin, Pinchas Lapide . . . Rabbi Alan Mittleman coined the phrase the "homecoming of Jesus."[4]

Perhaps the questions about Jesus' Jewishness can only be solved by Christians and Jews *together*—and therefore can lead to true dialogue. Do we really know what it means to be a Jew? Can we decide all by ourselves what is typically Jewish? What kind of Judaism are we speaking about? Is it possible for us today to reply to the questions, "To what degree is/was Jesus a Jew? What

---

[1] Minneapolis: Fortress Press, 1981.

[2] *Das christliche Bekenntnis zu Jesus dem Juden: Eine Christologie* (Gütersloh, 1992).

[3] J. H. Charlesworth, ed. (New York: Crossroad, 1991).

[4] "Beginning with Moses Mendelssohn and his contemporaries, Jewish writers were already departing from the caricatures of Jesus that their medieval predecessors had favored and were discovering in him instead 'a like-minded Jew.' Jesus, Mittlemarl says, has been in a sense 'returning to his ancestral home.' This homecoming is an important part of the modern discovery by Jews of their own history, an aspect of the current Jewish search for 'essence and definition.'" Quoted by Harvey Cox, "Jesus and Generation X," in *Jesus at 2000*, ed. Marcus Borg (Boulder, CO: Westview Press, 1998). Available online at http://www.urantiabook.org/J2000.htm (accessed September 4, 2008).

kind of Jew was he?" without involving our elder brother in the dialogue, without letting him tell us how *he* understands himself? Therefore, in what follows I will pay close attention to the many varieties of Judaism that have appeared over the course of twenty centuries. We Christians will still be asking *our* questions, but we will remain receptive to the often very different sensibilities of *the other* who is also dealing with these same questions.

Are the questions simply ones of curiosity, questions about history or exegesis? The second question suggests this: what kind of Jew *was* he? We love to amass knowledge, and in this way we are typical romantics. A good number of Westerners, Christians as well as Jews, share the romantic's desire to reconstruct what happened in the past in order to become in some way contemporary with it. It is certainly legitimate to treat Jesus and his history this way,[5] but we need to recognize that such an approach is not sufficient to establish Christian identity or to support a meaningful dialogue with our Jewish partners. So let us begin by dealing with these questions in terms of historical-critical research. We will then look at the different ways the Jewish people thought about the messiah in the centuries since the time of Jesus. Finally, we will return to the question of dialogue between these two great traditions in terms of Jesus space.

How Jewish Was Jesus? What Kind of a Jew Was He?

J. Leipoldt, a very learned German professor in the first half of the twentieth century, was still able to conclude, on the basis of

---

[5] When Edward Schillebeeckx finished his first book on Jesus—*Jesus, an Experiment in Christology* (New York: Seabury Press, 1979)—he admitted to me that the entire thesis of the book may have been out of date, even an exercise in romanticism, similar to those nineteenth-century endeavors to produce a critical history of Jesus. Nevertheless, he was determined to make one more attempt because he was convinced that with modern exegetical methods it would be possible to arrive at a historically solid and trustworthy conclusion.

his exegetical and historical research, that Jesus must have been born of a non-Jewish mother and therefore was not a Jew. In the genealogy of the first chapter of the Gospel of Matthew, Mary, the mother of Jesus, appears as the fifth and last woman. Now what did these five women have in common? According to Luther, the first four were sinners, and the reason they are listed among Jesus' ancestors is to show that he was born to "save his people from their sins" (see Matt 1:21). According to Leipoldt, these women—Tamar, Rahab, Ruth, and Bathsheba—were all pagans; therefore Mary must have been one too. (Be forewarned: erudition is a donkey you can hitch up to any wagon you want!)

Today no one doubts that Jesus was a Jew by birth, by education, and by culture. Jesus thought like a Jew, employing the thought patterns proper to his time and place. To do this, he must have assimilated a good bit of Jewish culture. Here are some examples to show the truly Jewish character of the person of Jesus.

The eighth chapter of the Gospel of John has preserved the account of an adulterous woman caught *in flagrante*. According to the law of Moses, she was to be stoned. The woman is brought to Jesus, and he is asked what is to be done in such a case. In fact, they want to know how he would interpret the law of Moses and how he would apply it in this particular situation (the Halakah).

In order to understand Jesus' response, one needs to be familiar with the rabbinical instructions on the way to carry out a stoning. (Yes, even for stoning there are rules to follow, preserved down to the present day in the Mishnah, which was put into writing around the year 200 CE.) First of all it is recommended that the person be thrown into a well and that stones be hurled from above. The first to cast their stones are the "sinners," those whose hands are dirty. The "righteous" are thereby dispensed. Knowing this, it is possible to understand the role of Saul at the stoning of Stephen. The reason those who stoned Stephen laid their garments at the feet of Saul was because he was "righteous," a strict observer of the law, and thus was not allowed to engage in this kind of activity. He did, nonetheless, fully approve of what was being done (Acts 7:58–8:1).

Now, what did Jesus say to those who insisted that he give his opinion about the case at hand? He turned the rules upside down, thereby demolishing the whole system: "Let anyone among you who is without sin be the first to throw a stone at her!" (John 8:7). In order to speak like this, he had to have detailed knowledge of the legal system and be able to move around in it freely.

In another place Jesus asks a rhetorical question: "If one of you has a child or an ox that has fallen into a well, will you not immediately pull it out on a sabbath day?" (Luke 14:5). The question has to do with the sacrosanct law of Sabbath rest. Jesus has been denounced as a transgressor of the law; he has just cured a sick person in the synagogue on the Sabbath. Jesus asks, "If one of you . . ." The question is direct and, to use a technical rhetorical term, *ad hominem*. But for those who have an up-to-date knowledge of the rules as well as the exceptions that are allowed, it is clear that Jesus is doing more than simply suggesting an analogous situation to his questioners. Jesus is referring to rules that are currently in force. More precisely, Jesus shows that he is aligning himself with the position of the Pharisees and distancing himself from the interpretation of the law that can be found in the manuscripts discovered at Qumran. There we read that it is strictly forbidden to pull an ass or an ox out of a well on the Sabbath. The Pharisees, noted for their more lenient approach to the law, were the only group to allow an exception to the law of Sabbath rest in the case of an animal that fell into a well (see Matt 12:11; also Luke 14:5 and 13:15). Jesus is therefore addressing himself to the Pharisees, expressing his agreement with their principles of interpretation, and showing that he is not at all supportive of the position of those who want to be more pious than all the rest. Jesus' teaching on the Sabbath can only be fully understood if it is put into the context of the many different legal opinions of the day.[6]

[6] In the Talmud and down to the present day, the teaching on the Sabbath has undergone such a striking evolution that we should be very careful about projecting back into the time of Jesus what only developed much later. See the wonderful contemporary work of Abraham Heschel, *The*

The evangelists frequently show Jesus being interrogated by the scribes and doctors of the law with regard to the commandments. On more than one occasion they ask, what in your mind is the greatest commandment? It is important to have a good understanding—in Jewish terms!—of this kind of question. When someone asks a question like this, he wants to know how the teacher organizes his thought, how he prioritizes his instructions. The purpose is not to be able to fulfill one commandment and neglect the rest, because *all* the commandments and precepts are to be kept (see Matt 23:23). Rather, in the event there is a conflict between two precepts, the response of the teacher will make it possible to choose the better course. In the Talmud one can find a whole host of responses to this one question (see especially the tractate *Makkoth* 23b–24a).

The First Testament already gives a number of responses to this question, and that fact is in itself quite instructive. Leviticus, the middle book of the Torah, gravitates around the law of holiness and repeats, "Be holy, for I the LORD your God am holy." In the book of Deuteronomy, "Hear, O Israel!" is repeated like a refrain. And then come the imperatives, all more or less equivalent and interchangeable: "You shall love the LORD your God"; "The LORD your God you shall fear; him you shall serve"; etc. (Deut 6:5, 13). In Genesis the first commandment addressed to the man and the woman is "Be fruitful and multiply" (1:28). The first prohibition appears in Genesis 2: "You shall not eat of this tree!" And in the list of the Ten Words—which Christians refer to as the "Ten Commandments" (see Exod 20 and Deut 5)—there are many commandments implicit in "You shall not kill," which can be considered the commandment par excellence

---

Sabbath: Its Meaning for Modern Man (New York: Farrar, Straus and Giroux, 1951). The same must be said with regard to the concept of the "Torah," generally understood as "Law," or of the "messiah." Knowledge of later traditions can sometimes facilitate the understanding of formulations that are much older but can also lead to ridiculous and even appalling anachronisms.

(note, for example, how much someone like Emmanuel Levinas emphasizes this commandment).

This first set of passages, taken entirely from the Torah of Moses, can be augmented with statements made by the prophets, beginning, for example, with Micah, who summarizes the whole law in a threefold command: "He has told you, O mortal, what is good; and what does the LORD require of you but to do justice, and to love kindness, and to walk humbly with your God?" (6:8). The prophet Hosea proclaims, "For I desire steadfast love and not sacrifice, the knowledge of God rather than burnt-offerings" (6:6). In the Talmud one can see how these words, along with some others, are cited to enhance the response given to the question about the first commandment, thereby keeping open the debate.[7]

The New Testament does the same thing, providing several responses and thereby obliging us to continue reflecting on the question. Here are a few examples:

- The first commandment is "Honor your father and mother" (Eph 6:2; see Mark 7:10).

- The first commandment is "You shall not murder" (Matt 5:21, at the beginning of six antitheses).

- The first commandment is "Hear, O Israel . . ." (see Mark 12:29; in Mark "hear" precedes the double commandment of love! But that is not the case in the parallel passages in Matthew and Luke).

---

[7] *Makkoth* 23b–24a begins with Moses and the 613 precepts, of which 365 are negative, like the number of days in a year; 248 are positive, like the number of organs in the human body, implying that one learns to serve God with all the time and all the space available. Then one moves on to David, who in Psalm 15 mentions eleven commandments that one must follow to dwell on the holy mountain of the Lord and in his tent. Then we come to Isaiah, who succeeds in reducing the commandments to six (see Isa 33:15f). Micah comes next with his threefold precept (see Mic 6:8, cited above). A reduction to two commandments is found in Isaiah 56:1. And finally one finds the entire Torah and the Prophets summarized in just one precept, Habakkuk's ". . . the righteous live by their faith" (2:4).

- The first commandment is "strive for his [God's] kingdom" and all the rest will follow (thus in Luke 12:31; compare with Matt 6:33).

- The first commandment is "Do to others as you would have them do to you" (Luke 6:31; Matt 7:12).

- The first commandment is "Be perfect" (Matt 5:48). "Be merciful" (Luke 6:36). "[B]e holy" (1 Pet 1:15-16).

- The first commandment is "You shall love the Lord your God . . . You shall love your neighbor as yourself" (see Matt 22:36-40; see also Luke 10:27, where it is a lawyer who brings together these two commandments!). For Paul all the Torah is summed up in the phrase "Love your neighbor as yourself" (Rom 13:9; see also Gal 5:14. This commandment is also found in Jas 2:8!).

To think like a Jew means first of all that we always keep in mind this range of responses. The final statement is the one we are most familiar with: the law is ultimately about love. But in his response (see Matt 22:36f and Mark 12:29f) Jesus goes further by engaging in a typically Jewish reflection. Rather than simply giving a response based on one passage of Scripture, he connects two texts taken from the Torah of Moses, Deuteronomy 6:5 and Leviticus 19:18: "You shall love the LORD your God with all your heart, and with all your soul, and with all your might" and "You shall not take vengeance or bear a grudge against any of your people, but you shall love your neighbor as yourself: I am the LORD." In Hebrew these two commandments begin with the exact same expression: *wĕʾāhabtā* (and you-will-love). According to Jewish hermeneutics you can always explain two texts that contain the same turn of phrase by using one to elucidate the other. And that is exactly what Jesus does here. He connects the first commandment about love of God with the second about love of neighbor, which he declares to be "equal to the first." Love of God is to be given concrete expression in love of the neighbor; love of neighbor demands a commitment as absolute as the commandment to love God "with all your heart, and with all your soul, and with all your might." One commandment completes the other.[8]

These few examples can suffice to show that Jesus thinks like a Jew and is to be regarded as one. Jesus and his questioners share a common culture, not only very Jewish, but very rabbinical as well.

The way the gospels were written also presupposes a Jewish worldview. Just one example. One cannot fully understand the first ten verses of the oldest gospel that has come down to us—that of Mark—without having recourse to some specifically Jewish hermeneutical tools.

Mark opens his gospel by citing a passage he attributes to Isaiah. What he has actually done, however, is put together Malachi 3:1 and Exodus 23:20 and then skillfully joined them to Isaiah 40:3 by using the technique, described above, of relating different texts that contain the same turn of phrase. In this way the evangelist achieves a triple identification:

- God addresses himself to a "you" who comes on the scene like a new Moses. In Exodus 23:20 God promises Moses that he will "send an angel in front of you." The "you" here can only be Jesus, the new Moses who is to come (see Deuteronomy 18:15, 18, which Mark cites further on).

- The "angel in front of you" is John the Baptist, introduced in verse four and endowed in verse six with the attributes of Elijah. According to Malachi 3:1, 23, Elijah is the precursor of the Messiah.

- Finally, it is apparent that the reference in Isaiah 40 to the "way" that is to be prepared in the desert is the way of *the Lord* himself.

---

[8] A modern concordance makes it possible to confirm that in the entire Torah of Moses there are only three passages that begin with the phrase *wĕʾāhabtā*: Deuteronomy 6:5; Leviticus 19:18; and Leviticus 19:34 ("and you will love him as yourself"—referring to the foreigner). The expression is rare and thus lends itself to being interpreted in the light of its use in other passages.

It follows that Jesus is the second Moses; he is the one who comes after Elijah, the precursor; he is the Messiah; he is the Lord himself!

When read in their wider context, Exodus 23, Isaiah 40, and Malachi 3 all refer to the exodus, and more precisely, to a new exodus that will be final and definitive.

Mark thus begins his account of Jesus by carefully employing the sophisticated hermeneutic of the midrashic schools to introduce John on the stage of human history.

A few verses further on we read that "John was clothed with camel's hair, with a leather belt around his waist" (Mark 1:6). This description of his garments clearly refers back to the description of Elijah in the first chapter of the second book of Kings. There the king asks the messengers, "'What sort of man was he who came to meet you and told you these things?' They answered him, 'A hairy man, with a leather belt around his waist.' He said, 'It is Elijah the Tishbite'" (2 Kgs 1:7-8). Anyone familiar with this text would see in Mark's seemingly incidental description of John's clothing a direct confirmation of what was already indicated by the earlier reference to Malachi's prophecy: John is this Elijah who was to come! (Mark 1:2-3; see 9:11-13).

When John speaks, he uses expressions that would be immediately intelligible in the Jewish setting of that time, but which might appear obscure or even indecipherable to a contemporary reader. He says, "[T]he one who [is more powerful than I] is coming after me; I am not worthy to untie the thong of his sandal" (John 1:27). The phrase "coming after me" means that he has a follower, a disciple. "[N]ot worthy to untie the thong of his sandal" is a technical expression for work that was reserved to slaves. Rabbinical literature forbade a teacher to order his disciple to undo his sandal straps. He had to treat his disciple as a disciple and not as a slave. The meaning of John's words, then, is "I have a disciple who is much greater than his master. Not only am I not worthy to be *his* disciple but I am not even worthy to be his slave! That is how great the disciple is who is coming after me!" By means of figurative speech and the use of exaggeration, John clearly indicates how he regards the longed-for-one who is appearing on the horizon.

In the following verse (Mark 1:9) we read what appears to be little more than a throwaway comment: "And it came to pass in those days, Jesus came from Nazareth of Galilee." This chain of commonplace expressions ("it came to pass," "in those days," "Jesus came") corresponds word for word to the first part of Exodus 2:11.[9] There it is the adult Moses who is spoken of: "And it cometh to pass, in those days, that Moses is grown, and he goeth out unto his brethren."[10] The literary methods of the scribes and catechists of the time drew heavily on such textual similarities. In this case what Mark is saying is "As was the first Moses, so will be the last," paralleling the rabbinic saying "As was the first savior, so will be the last." As Moses was, so will the Messiah be.

This line of thought can be continued. In Exodus 2:11 Moses comes and observes that his brothers are suffering, crushed by forced labor. Jesus comes to the Jordan, where John is plunging those who confess their sins into the water. Both Moses and Jesus humble themselves in an act of solidarity that will flower in liberation. One who writes like this also wants to be read like this.

Jesus himself and an evangelist like Mark think, speak, write, and reason like Jews. The more we become familiar with their Jewish cultural location, the more we will be able to understand their way of speaking, their figures of speech, their rhetoric, and their logic. However, this is not to say that everything has to correspond to what is thought or felt in this particular cultural setting. In many ways Jesus and Mark separate themselves from their milieu, but even when they do, they use the language of those they are addressing. For example, when Jesus indicates

[9] This similarity was first noted by Marie-Emile Boismard more than forty years ago. A computer search can now confirm that nowhere else in the Torah will one find this juxtaposition of "it came to pass," "in those days," and "came."

[10] This translation of both verses, that from Mark and that from Exodus, is from "Young's Literal Translation," found online at http://www.biblegateway.com (accessed August 25, 2008).

that he does not want to be recognized as a rabbi but as a prophet (Mark 11:17–12:12), the distinction he makes is immediately understood.

The question still remains, however: historically speaking, how far did this break go? Was it already irreversible at the time of Jesus? Even though we may not be able to rewrite history, we can still try to determine what it was that tilted the balance and created the radical opposition on both sides that led to a complete break in the course of the second century.

Filling Out Our Knowledge of the History of the Other

Many Christians, upon learning that the gospels present a Jesus who was profoundly marked by Jewish thought and customs, are surprised that he was so little known, recognized, or respected by his fellow Jews. Sometimes their surprise masks an element of indignation.

But if we think like this, we should not forget just *who* these fellow Jews really were and are. Our surprise shows that we have lost sight of them and their history. For many Christians Jewish history ends with the death of Jesus on Golgotha in the year 30 or 33. They know absolutely nothing about the growth and spiritual development of the Jewish people after that. So we need to take some time to learn how the Jews continued to deal with the concept of a messiah and how their profound and revitalized insights continue to make it very difficult for them to recognize Jesus as the Messiah or the Anointed One of the end time.

When we look at Jewish history from the time of Herod the Great and the beginnings of the Christian movement down to the present, we see that messianic expectations developed along two different lines.[11] The first trajectory shows how Jewish belief was organized

---

[11] I rely here on the influential work of Gershom Scholem, *Major Trends of Jewish Mysticism* (New York: Schocken Books, 1995). The work originally appeared in 1950.

in order to protect itself against certain messianic and apocalyptic ideas of a revolutionary nature; the second trajectory traces the eruptions of messianic fervor over the course of centuries.

Jewish Responses to Revolutionary Messianism

With regard to the first trajectory, four moments stand out in this long history of Jewish reflection.

Around the year 200 of the Common Era, the great rabbinic master Yehuda the Prince (Ha-Nassi) composed the Mishnah, an extraordinary compilation of the traditions that regulate every action (the Halakah) of the pious Jew. The overarching purpose of this impressive tractate—think of it as the bible for religious practice alongside the great Hebrew Bible—is to create a Judaism *without* a messiah, a Judaism free of all eschatological tension, cut off from any apocalyptic tendencies. Rabbi Yehuda and his colleagues kept their distance from every kind of nationalistic struggle against Rome, or any other political entity, for that matter. Their Judaism was first and foremost vertical, consisting in the scrupulous observance of all the many precepts. "They [the precepts] will preserve the bond between you and the Most High and will assure you a place on this earth." Everyone still remembered how resistance against the Romans, first against Vespasian and Titus (between 66 and 73) and then against Hadrian (132–35), had ended in crushing defeat.

The Talmud was composed in stages between the third and eighth centuries and is basically a systematic commentary on and complement to Rabbi Yehuda's Mishnah. It exists in two versions: the Palestinian, also referred to as the Talmud of Jerusalem, and the Babylonian, which is more developed and more widely known. Many traditions that had been discarded now reappear and once again become material for debate and reflection. In the Talmud everything is subject to debate, even apocalyptic themes like the resurrection of the dead or the coming of the messiah. This does not yet mean that one can depart even a little from any of the norms and rules given in the Mishnah;

in practice, everything that was prescribed is to be observed. But the debate surrounding each question is broadened; every position is open to reexamination, even those that had been dispensed with. The horizon is widened and deepened.

The fundamental tendency of the Talmud is to make sure that every question is exhaustively analyzed by subjecting it to all the contradictory opinions that had previously been brought forth. The task of the student—the *talmid*—is to continue to ruminate on these questions while taking new situations into account. This kind of highly dialectic reflection has become the model for the practice of teaching and learning down to the present day. Thus it is that faith in the resurrection is founded on references taken from the three parts of biblical revelation: the Torah, the Prophets, and the Writings. But the same section of the Talmud gives voice to those who contest the resurrection by also appealing to the law of Moses, to Ezekiel or Hosea, and to one or the other psalm. One is therefore permitted to believe in the resurrection, but it cannot be said that resurrection is a defined doctrine, one that has been approved by the masters.

By the same token, the coming of the messiah is at one and the same time the best and the worst of things that can be anticipated, the most certain of things to come and the least clear, an event for which you can prepare (as you would prepare for a scorpion bite!), something present everywhere (even in the very name of your master), but never able to be discerned with certitude. Anyone who scrutinizes the teaching of the masters on the coming of the messiah learns what it means to be expectant and skeptical at the same time, to be without illusions but not completely abandon messianism, which Emmanuel Levinas referred to as the lever of history.[12]

---

[12] Emmanuel Levinas devoted two conferences to the problem of the messiah, commenting on the last chapter of the tractate Sanhedrin (98b–99a) of the Babylonian Talmud. See *Difficile liberté: Essai sur le judaïsme* (Paris: Albin Michel, 1963), pp. 83–131. Marcel Poorthuis made a detailed study of these commentaries of Levinas. See his thesis *Het gelaat van de messias* (The face of the messiah): *Messiaanse talmoedlezingen van Emmanuel Levinas; Vertaling,*

In order to see how this kind of reflection is carried out, we will examine in some detail one sentence from the Talmud: "Rav said that the world was created for David alone, and Samuel said that it was created for Moses. As for Rabbi Johanan, he said that the world was created for the messiah alone" (Sanhedrin 98a). Here we have three authoritative statements but no dogmatic pronouncement on the subject. How are we to understand "David" in relation to "Moses," or the "messiah" in relation to the other two? "Moses" can be understood as the name for a way of life that is based on the Torah and conforms to the rules of the Halakah. It is the way of wisdom taught by the rabbis and the Pharisees. "David," on the other hand, represents another view of life, one dedicated to praise, to the temple, to the cultic dimension of human existence revered by the priestly tradition. It corresponds to the ancient ideal of the Sadducees. If the human being in the image of "Moses" is the wise and ethically responsible person, the human being in the image of "David" is the priest, the celebrant at the heart of creation. Rabbi Johanan then looks toward the future, to the coming of the messiah, the anointed one at the end of the ages, the one announced by the prophets. No one is obliged to accept any of these proposals, nor to exclude any one of them. They call us to reflect. If I opt for one of the three, I should not forget that the other two also help to clarify the meaning of my existence. The priestly vision of "David," the prophetic vision of the "messiah," and the sapiential vision of "Moses" are complementary and balance one another. And if someone does not believe in the possibility that the messiah will come, that does not make him a despicable heretic.

---

commentaar, achtergronden (Hilversum: Folkertsma Stichting voor Talmudica, 1993). The debate about each question is still open, as the Talmud teaches us. See also Elie Wiesel, *Célébration talmudique* (Paris: Seuil, 1991), who brings an original point of view to these open questions.

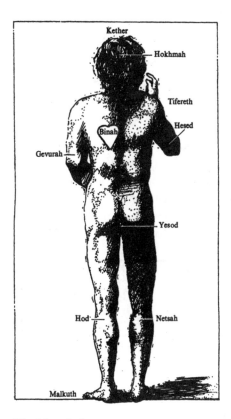

Kether

Hokhmah

Tifereth

Binah

Hesed

Gevurah

Yesod

Hod

Netsah

Malkuth

The Adam Qadmon

The Kabbalah, the *Adam Qadmon*, and the Hassidic Movement

In the eighth and ninth centuries a new reading of the entire tradition took shape. Known as the Kabbalah, it is a fundamentally new system, though it does include ancient traditions that left some traces in the Talmud. Concern about history and about possible messianic revolutions passes into the background. Life takes the form of a vertical ladder. The Nameless One is located beyond the highest echelon. Ten spheres (*sefirot*), ten "names of God," ten attributes come one after the other in a descending pattern, like so many emanations of the Invisible, the Infinite (*En Sof*). At the tenth echelon the kingdom comes to be established on earth. The three superior spheres are only slightly distinguished from the seven inferior ones, and these are also associated with the seven days of the week. You can either go up this ladder or down it. In all its parts it corresponds to the first Man, *Adam Qadmon*, the one who was created in the image of God according to Genesis (1:27) and now bears that image. The three spheres are also arranged in three columns. The right column contains the attributes of largesse, love, and universality; the left the attributes of rigor, law, and particularity; the central pillar is made up of the four attributes of equilibrium: the crown, mercy (which also includes beauty), justice (or the foundation), and the kingdom.

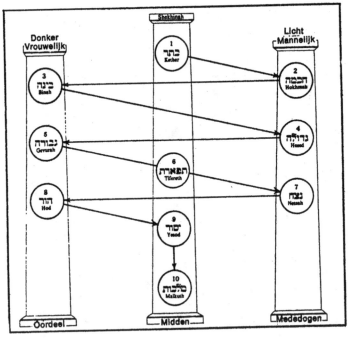

The sepherotic tree arranged in three columns

We are here in the presence of a vast and rigorous system that encompasses all history, all human experience, the entire cosmos.

When we regard it more closely, we see that it dispenses with any notion of mediation or of an appeal that is rooted in history. It can thus be thought of as a "Christology without Christ." Not all Jewish teachers today are familiar with this Kabbalistic system, but it has left its influence everywhere, even in the way one interprets the most minute liturgical gestures, chooses the proper color for a feast day, etc.

The last transformation of Jewish thought began in central Europe in the eighteenth century with the advent of the modern Hassidic movement, a charismatic movement with many branches and with offshoots down to the present day. It emphasizes anthropology and the spiritual liberty of every observant Jew (the *hassid*). Here too messianic expectation is revolutionized to such a degree that the messiah is no longer located outside oneself or in some other place. "I am the messiah" becomes the ordinary way of expressing messianism. I am directly responsible for his coming. Each person has the lofty responsibility of making manifest his auspicious silhouette. Every pregnant woman deserves to be greeted as if she carried the presence of him who is the object of messianic hope.

This second line of development identified by Gershom Scholem over the course of twenty centuries of history contains two moments that I would like to highlight.

During the second revolt against Rome (from 132 to 135), Rabbi Akiva, one of the most renowned masters of that period, designated the military chief and political leader of the revolt as *the* messiah. He gave him the name of Bar Kochba, meaning "son of the star," referring to the messianic star of the prophecy found in Numbers 24:17: "[A] star shall come out of Jacob, and a scepter shall rise out of Israel" (see Matt 2:1f.). The great expectation that accompanied this title—an expectation, however, not shared by all—was viciously crushed by the Roman armies. Bar Kochba was killed, Rabbi Akiva was tortured to death, the holy city Jerusalem was turned into a Roman military camp called Aelia Capitolina, and its temple and courtyard were utterly destroyed and desecrated. A temple dedicated to Jupiter Capitolinus was erected on the esplanade. It is from this period that the Western Wall, also known as the Wailing Wall, was set apart as a privileged place of prayer for the Jewish people. It was part of the temple built by Herod and supported the courtyard of the temple and its western foundation. The identification of Bar Kochba as the messiah and the violent repression launched by the emperor Hadrian continue to traumatize the collective memory of the Jewish people down to the present day.

The Christians of the time, even those of Jewish origin, were unable to accept this military hero proclaimed as the messiah and savior, because their paschal faith already recognized Jesus as Messiah and Lord. The concurrence of these two messiahs and the war of repression were responsible for putting an even greater distance between these two communities and traditions.

Another profoundly traumatic moment for the messianic expectations of the Jewish people appeared in the person of a Talmudic and Kabbalistic scholar, Sabbatai Zevi (1626–76). At first, recognition of his messianic identity was confined to the circle of his disciples, but in the summer of 1665 Zevi met Nathan of Gaza, who identified Zevi as the messiah and declared himself his prophet. In December of that same year, in the synagogue of Smyrna, his native city, Sabbatai Zevi openly declared himself to be king and messiah, creating turmoil in the entire Jewish world of the time. He set out for Constantinople, where he was taken prisoner and handed over to the sultan. In the end he became a Muslim. Most Jews were terribly confused and scandalized, but some of his most ardent disciples remained faithful, convinced that his conversion to Islam was part of a mysterious divine plan. Relegated to a little village in Albania, he died in complete obscurity.

Remnants of Sabbataism could be found in Europe and America up until the nineteenth century, and even today the Dönmeh sect continues to exist within Turkish Islam. Outwardly it is Muslim, but it is actually a covert Jewish sect that remains faithful to Sabbatai Zevi.

A disciple by the name of Jacob Frank (1726–91) played an especially influential role within Sabbataism. He considered himself the immediate successor of the founder and preached a doctrine of total liberty flowing from mystical faith in this messiah. He was not attracted to Islam but to Catholicism, receiving baptism in the cathedral church of Warsaw with the emperor August III as his godfather. The following year he was accused of witchcraft, imprisoned for thirteen years, and venerated as the "suffering messiah." Later he took up residence in Offenbach, near Frankfurt, secretly directed the sect of his followers, and continued to practice orgiastic rituals. A century later Frankism spread as far as America.

The colossal collapse of Sabbataism continues to be a topic for reflection among scholars and historians of Jewish mysticism, who ask how such a movement could ever have arisen and spread. Some have tried to find an explanation by recalling the situation of the Jews in Spain and Portugal during the course of the fourteenth and fifteenth centuries. In order to survive persecution and the Inquisition, a good many Jews formally accepted Christianity but remained clandestine Jews. They were referred to as the Marranos. Exteriorly and culturally they were Christians, but interiorly and spiritually they continued to be faithful Jews. On the basis of this double belonging—already known in the Greek period, as attested to by the book of Judith in the Greek Bible—a rationale was worked out that Sabbatai Zevi then developed into a coherent system. He and his disciple Jacob Frank included some ethical principles taken from the Talmudic tradition. The Talmud taught that "the messiah would come in a generation that was totally just or totally perverse." Through their own perverse reworking of this text, they held that all rules of conduct were suspended. "Since the first possible occurrence has not taken place, we have to do what we can to bring the second to pass, and then the messiah will come," they said. "Since we are unable to be saints, let us be sinners, and then redemption will take place." "Let the eradication of the Torah become its true fulfillment."

Be that as it may, this huge setback, with all the confusion, scandal, and shame that it brought, had a much greater impact on messianic thought in official rabbinical circles than the failure of Bar Kochba. It should not be surprising that Frankism, whose leader had been baptized a Catholic, made rapprochement with the Christian tradition all the more difficult.[13]

If we now consider both lines of development as described by Gershom Scholem, we have to admit that Jewish messianic thought, independent of any reference to Jesus, was exceedingly complex, made up of both enthusiastic messianic currents and strongly antimessianic tendencies. Jews have known more than one messianic awakening, and the three great periods of creative thought (Talmudic, Kabbalistic, and Hassidic), each in its own way, tried to counter the danger while preserving the fervor of these movements. It is from the *inside* of this rich "messianic" discussion that we Christians, with our two-thousand-year-old formula "Jesus is (for us) the Messiah," want to enter into dialogue with the Jewish people. The first step may well be to accept the fact that such a desire will evoke very little, if any, positive response. In fact, we may find ourselves wondering if they understand what we are talking about, even though we are using a word that we always have had and still have in common: the *messiah*.

After the Twentieth Century

The events of the twentieth century, including the significant developments that took place in the second half of the century, have placed great obstacles in the way of Christians who want to be reconciled with their older brother.

There is almost no one left who remembers what Jewish-Christian relations were like in the Jewish communities of Europe before the advent of Nazism. A Jewish confrere of mine,

---

[13] These two notable examples of messianic figures in the history of the Jewish people are by no means the only ones. Among many others, who are sometimes treated as pseudo-messiahs, we can mention Abu Issa al-Isfahani and his disciple Yudghan in the eighth century, David Alroy (Persia, twelfth century), and Abraham Aboulafia (Spain, thirteenth century). See Moshe Idel, *L'Expérience mystique d'Abraham Aboulafia* (Paris: Cerf, 1989).

Fr. Cosmas Hamburger, was born in Silesia in 1890, worked as a doctor in Berlin, and converted to Christianity in 1919. He was the last of his family to do so. His brother, the philosopher Siegfried-Benedict, friend of Dietrich von Hildenbrand, was baptized together with Edith Stein. "As Jews we were inevitably turned toward Christ," Fr. Cosmas recalled sixty years later, and this "we" meant much more than his immediate family.[14] Describing the period before the First World War, Max Nordau, a colleague of Theodore Herzl at the beginning of the Zionist movement, wrote, "Jesus is the soul of our soul, just as he is flesh of our flesh. Who would want to separate him from the Jewish people?" Such openness is also to be found in the writings of Franz Rosenzweig, especially in *The Star of Redemption*.[15]

But everything changed after the rise of Nazism and the slaughter of six million Jews. There are Jewish thinkers today, Stephane Moses or F. Schlegel, for example, who reproach Rosenzweig for not having foreseen—much less given warning of—the onset of the Shoah. The Shoah has indeed inflicted grievous wounds on the Judeo-Christian relationship. Some Christians are puzzled by the often indignant reaction of Jews to the canonization of Edith Stein. Jews, for their part, find it difficult to accept the spiritual legacy of Etty Hillesum, even though she was and remained Jewish. For Christians, on the other hand, she has become a witness who is read and appreciated almost without reserve.

The Shoah itself can be read in different ways. One reading stresses the fact that those who ordered and carried out this extermination of the Jewish people were all baptized Christians. For some this is evidence of Christian anti-Semitism. Even

[14] Especially helpful for understanding Jewish life in Europe between 1900 and 1950 is the biographical sketch of Marcel Poorthuis and Theo Salemink, *Op zoek naar de blauwe ruiter: Sophie van Leer, een leven tussen avant garde, jodendom en christendom (1892–1953)* (Nijmegen: Valkhof Pers, 2000).

[15] *The Star of Redemption*, trans. Barbara E. Galli (Madison: University of Wisconsin Press, 2005).

though not everyone interprets the same evidence the same way, and even though differences can be found on both the individual and collective levels, still, for the sake of encounter, it is important that Christians be aware that a good number of Jews interpret the Shoah this way. That awareness will help us understand that many Jews will simply not be able to tolerate any reference to Jesus as a Jewish messiah, and therefore their savior too. How can Jews be expected to place their faith in the God of their persecutors? How can they be expected to see in this "Jesus crucified" the fulfillment of the messianic promises, when the followers of this Jesus, acting in his name, persecuted them, crucified them, and did so century after century, down to the present generation?

The twentieth century was witness to a second important event for the dialogue between Christians and Jews, the foundation of the State of Israel three years after the end of the Second World War (1948). Statehood represents a completely new political identity in the history of the Jewish people, and this event has a specifically *messianic* character for them. After twenty centuries of exile, the reestablishment of a relationship between the people and the land signifies something new in history, something with messianic overtones. This relationship continues to be attacked from the outside, and even internally there are different points of view because of conflicting ideological positions. All the while the territories that are under military surveillance are subject to constant warfare.

Be that as it may, we still have to pay attention to the reality of the situation. To what degree are we, Christians of Gentile stock, capable of understanding the messianism of this new political entity called Israel? This messianism is clearly different from ours, but are we only capable of understanding what is ours or what is similar to it? Even in purely political discussions it seems that we, as Westerners (and as Christians), have too little respect for the spiritual self-understanding of the Jewish people. For them, being reconnected with the land is part and parcel of their divine election and a sign of God's covenant with them. This point of view is quite novel, but might it be something that we too could accept and respect? We should be able to advance the strictly political debate—justly balancing rights and duties vis-à-vis the other population dwelling in the same country—while respecting the messianic self-understanding of the Jews.

Finally, we need to consider two more recent events that make the Christian assertion that Jesus is the Messiah particularly difficult for Jews to accept.

First of all there is the fact that another messiah was made known not too long ago. The person this time was Menachem Mendel Schneerson, the great teacher and rabbi of the Chabad-Lubavitch movement, who was recognized and proclaimed as the messiah shortly after his death in 1994. Let us recall that the foundation of the State of Israel is explicitly extolled in prayer by the rabbinate as "the herald of the approach of our deliverance." When a certain charismatic group proclaims someone as a messianic figure, such a proclamation takes place within a global context of waiting for redemption that is now tied to the reality of an independent state.

Something else has also come from America, a new movement called "Jews for Jesus." These Jews recognize Jesus as the Messiah, but they are not thus far connected with any Christian church. The movement has now spread to Israel, to the great displeasure of the Orthodox Jews.

All these data create a world that Christians need to be aware of if they want to enter into some form of dialogue with the Jewish people. A significant change in our language and way of thinking about Jesus will be needed if we want to show respect for the other's position and to be able to communicate in a way that can be understood, at least to some degree.

* * *

> *Messianism is the lever of history.*
> —Emmanuel Levinas[16]

> *If it were possible to summarize the history of Israel in a single word*
> *and to reduce its contribution to one basic inspiration,*
> *we would not hesitate to say that the very essence of the people is hope.*
> —Benjamin Gross

> *In the house of Israel*
> *it has always been apocalyptic messianism,*
> *with its anarchist elements,*
> *that has brought a breath of fresh air.*
> *This messianism reminds us*
> *that history is burdened by catastrophes*
> *in a universe bereft of salvation.*
> —Gershom Scholem

The study of messianism has helped me understand how messianic hope functions. Too often our confession "Jesus is the Messiah" has given the impression that there is nothing more to wait or hope for. How can someone who has everything still hope for something? If I confess that I already have everything I could ever need and want, how will I be able to await something new, something even more beautiful than what I have already received? Messianism understood as a lever (Emmanuel Levinas) restores some enthusiasm to life by affirming that something more beautiful is still to come. The most beautiful messianic prophecies await their final fulfillment: the lion and the lamb

---

[16] In an article in which he reflects as a philosopher on the central mystery of Christianity, the humbling of God in the incarnation and the salvific substitution that takes place in the passion of Christ, Levinas arrives at this conclusion: "The 'I' is the one who, prior to any decision, is chosen to bear complete responsibility for the World. Messianism is this apogee in Being—a reversal of being that 'persists in its being'—which begins in me." In *Qui est Jésus-Christ? Semaine des intellectuels catholiques (6–13 mars 1968)* (Paris: Desclée de Brouwer, 1968), 192.

still do not eat side by side, the little child does not yet *p*_
the hole of the asp. The whole earth still waits to be "full of the
knowledge of the LORD as the waters cover the sea" (Isa 11:5-10).
Christian messianism, with its stress on the "already," is in danger of losing sight of the "not yet." The Jewish people may be
able to help us maintain the tension between the "already" and
the "not yet."[17]

Three Important Periods

To conclude, I would like to single out three moments in the
spiritual history of the Jewish people. I sincerely hope that Jesus
space will not be eradicated by encountering this history—nor
eradicate it—but rather that it will be expanded through our increased knowledge of the other and, God willing, the other's
increased knowledge of us.

With regard to the great period of the Mishnah and the Talmud, Jesus space and certain witnesses of early Hassidism need
to be placed side by side.

With regard to the Kabbalistic period, it will be helpful to
bring together Jesus space and the Sefirotic tree.

And finally, with regard to more recent times, it will certainly
be worthwhile to compare Rabbi Nahman of Bratslav with Jesus
and his space.

I will not be able to go into great detail in speaking of these
three encounters; rather, I will simply highlight their main
characteristics.

The first spiritual path has already been subjected to historical investigation by several authors, notably Geze Vermes

---

[17] In Christian churches it is only in the season of Advent that we read
the First Testament as a hope-filled promise that looks forward to a future
that has not yet come to pass, in spite of the coming of Jesus in history. In
Advent we learn, thanks to the liturgy, really *to hope*. But is Advent nothing
more than a liturgical season? Is it not rather the revelation of a fundamental
dimension of our existence, which is as human as it is Christian?

and Gerard F. Willems. Like Jesus, some Galilean rabbis were known as great miracle workers and friends of the poor. They also expressed their relationship to God in a manner that was direct, intimate, and full of confidence, regarding God like a father (*abba*) in heaven. More than anything else, their teaching emphasized just and generous behavior. A comparison of their statements and their brief narratives with the terse sayings and pronouncements of Jesus in the gospels indicates how much they have in common. Jesus needs to be understood within the well-defined context of the world of the Pharisees. By being situated in this concrete historical context, he is given another chance to be taken seriously and to find his place in the dialogue. He becomes less of an outsider to this great tradition. In this line we can appreciate the intuition that the exegete Fr. Jacques Dupuis formulated shortly before his death: What led the Christian movement to break with Judaism was not so much Christology, but a fundamental disagreement over Halakah, the concrete prescriptions that regulated the Jew's behavior vis-à-vis pagans. On this point the two parties were unable to agree.

Jesus space and the spiritual space in which the first Hassidic masters moved in the Judaism of that time have something to say to one another. A deeper understanding of these two complementary traditions has every chance of enabling Christians and Jews to move beyond mutual rejection and grow in mutual respect and even admiration for one another.

To be initiated into the world of the Kabbalah is to discover a space that binds heaven and earth. Originating from "the One who cannot be named," an immense space opens up in a descending movement of emanations, manifestations, and various "creations" and "births," finally taking concrete shape in what we see and are here and now. It is also possible to discover this space by climbing up the ladder of the ten *sefirot* or "spheres," each of which signifies a name, a property, or an attribute of God, and is identified with a patriarch. Thus, the seven last *sefirot* are identified with the following biblical figures: Abraham, Isaac and Jacob, Moses and Aaron, Joseph and David. As one moves up, the spheres become wider and wider. The smallest circle is at the bottom, while at the top one finds a circle without circumference, the *En Sof*, "that which has no end," the Infinite or the Unlimited.

All of this space is sometimes depicted as a tree that has its roots in heaven (a figure that one finds in Plato and in many spiritual traditions), sometimes as a human being, the androgynous Adam, the one from the very beginning, the Image of the Invisible, according to which we have all been created. In most drawings this figure of Adam is shown from behind. Moses, when he asked to see the glory of God, had already received this response: "you shall see my back . . . But . . . you cannot see my face; for no one shall see me and live." Is that not the precise moment when Moses understands the name of the Lord (Yhwh), who passes by and is given so many attributes? Those who meditate on the tree of the ten *sefirot* are able to partake of the knowledge of God that was granted to Moses at the high point of his encounter with God on Mount Sinai (Exod 33 and 34).

It seems to me that Christians whose lives are shaped by Jesus space and who become familiar with the spiritual dynamism of the Kabbalah are not taken out of their own territory but are challenged to be enriched by going more deeply into it. Jesus space refers us to the Jesus of history, and to much more than that. The Christ celebrated in the liturgy embraces heaven and earth and is confessed as the image of the invisible God, who bestows freedom, grace, justice, mercy, and the kingdom of peace in a descending movement that comes to fill our hearts, the lives of our communities, and our existing institutions.

The similarity between our understanding of Jesus space and what we find in the Kabbalah can be a source of spiritual growth. For example, on some occasions when I was part of a group of Christians and Jews who came together to read passages of the gospels or the letter of Paul, we found that we were able to make some remarkable discoveries together. The surprising parallels that we found were an indication that these two spaces—that of the Kabbalah and that of Christ—are not necessarily mutually exclusive but can in fact enrich each other. Here are a couple of examples to illustrate this point.

In the letter to the Colossians the author prays for those he is addressing:

> For this reason, since the day we heard it, we have not ceased praying for you and asking that you may be filled with the *knowledge* of God's *will* in all spiritual *wisdom* and *understanding*, so that you may lead lives worthy of the Lord, fully pleasing to him, as you bear fruit in every good work and as you grow in the knowledge of God. (1:9-10; italics added)

Those who have become familiar with the titles of the ten *sefirot*, who have learned to distinguish their relative position and their dynamic interaction, will immediately recognize that this prayer follows a descending pattern, starting from the highest *sefirah*, the *will*, (in Hebrew *ratzon*), followed by *wisdom* (*hokmah*), and then *understanding* (*binah*), the capacity to distinguish and comprehend (*syneis* in Greek). Beginning with these most prominent attributes, the prayer makes its way down to concrete acts, passing through the middle *sefirah*, the "sphere" of mercy and beauty, to arrive at the justice of the righteous and the kingdom on earth.

Following this descending movement, which is principally ethical and intended to shape the life of the Christian, is a hymn to Christ, expressed in a "doxological" ascending movement. Here Christ is presented as the "Image of the Invisible." He is thought to be at the beginning of everything that has come to be, similar to the *Adam Qadmon* of the Kabbalah. (*Qadmon* refers to what has been before—*qedem*—all time.) Christ is also recognized as the final fulfillment of all that exists: "For in him all the fullness of God was pleased to dwell" (Col 1:19). Here we are asked to consider the transition that begins with the one who is above every name and ends with the full stature of the first *sefirah*, characterized by the *will* ("was pleased"), the divine good pleasure (*ratzon* in Hebrew, *eudokia* in Greek). This unique stature contains the entire universe, both in the Kabbalah and in the fragment of this hymn: "through him God was pleased to reconcile to himself all things, whether on earth or in heaven, by making peace through the blood of his cross" ("all things," *ta panta* = the universe; Col 1:20).

The second example comes from the Gospel of Mark. The first person to come on stage is John the Baptist. His role is to introduce Jesus and to function as a *prologos* in the technical sense of the word. In classical Greek drama this performer was responsible for introducing the action in the name of the playwright and for placing before the spectators the real protagonist, the hero of the drama.

But the character of John is described variously. At the beginning three scriptural citations are joined together to tell us who he is and how we are to understand his relationship to Jesus. A little further on the narrator describes the kind of life he leads, giving us details about his clothing and his diet. Curiously, three animals are associated with this description: "Now John was clothed with camel's hair, with a leather belt around his waist, and he ate locusts and wild honey" (Mark 1:6). The first references to camel's hair and leather belt are, as we have seen, a literary recall of the figure of Elijah as he is described in 2 Kings 1:8. But there is more.

In rabbinic and Kabbalistic typology, the "camel" is associated with the fourth attribute, love, goodness, generosity (*hesed*). The grasshopper, on the other hand, because it devours everything (as we read in the first chapter of the prophecy of Joel), suggests rigor and is connected with the fifth attribute, *din*, or the rigor of the law. As for honey, which comes from the bee (Deborah), it is traditionally associated with the sixth attribute, beauty and mercy (*tiferet* and *rachamim*). In their sequence these three attributes indicate a descending movement.

Thus John, by his whole person as well as by his style of life, prepares the way for the coming of the "messiah king," of the "son of David," and of the "son of Joseph." The kingdom (*malkout*) forms the tenth and last *sefirah*, associated with the name of David. The ninth is that of Joseph, the just one. Gathering together in himself all these attributes, John prepares for the coming of the kingdom (Mark 1:14-15!), which is also the coming of the Holy Spirit (Mark 1:8, 11) and his indwelling in us (the *Shekinah*, also associated with the tenth and last *sefirah*). Thanks to these mani-fold allusions to the *sefirah*, the opening of the Gospel of Mark becomes a powerful expression of vertical communication ("the heavens [were] torn apart," Mark 1:10!) in order to make present the kingdom of God among us (see Mark 1:15).

All this may surprise us, but in the gospels Jesus himself, speaking to his disciples, puts forth this demand: if anyone wants to "enter the kingdom of God," it is necessary that the "camel . . . go through the eye of a needle" (see Mark 10:25). Here is the camel once again, the symbol of *hesed*, tradition-ally the virtue of those who are rich, generous, and hospitable, as was Abraham or Job. But the camel has to pass through an extremely narrow opening, "through the eye of a needle," if it wants to enter the kingdom. It has to pass through the gate of the next attribute, *din*, the rigor and severity of justice. Universal love will have to become concrete and particular. For this reason Abraham was put to the test one last time on Mount Moriah, where he learned to let go of his only son, Isaac. If Abraham is traditionally associated with the attribute of *hesed*, the name of Isaac is attached to *din*. Abraham, the universalist, is placed opposite Isaac, the particularist. After passing through *din*, the fifth attribute, one arrives at the attribute of mercy, love of the poor, the *sefirah* of Jacob. In the passage of the gospel that we are considering, the rich man who came to Jesus and so graciously greeted him as "Good Teacher" (*hesed* without *din*!) is exhorted to "sell what you own, and give the money to the poor" (Mark 10:17, 21). His graciousness has to pass through rigor in order to produce mercy for the poor. Because he is not able to navigate this passage, he closes himself off from what should follow, namely, entrance into the kingdom, which is the final *sefirah*.

In these three examples the exegetical methods of the Kabbal-ists were applied to three typically Christian texts. We should note that in all three cases the movement is first of all a descend-ing one. These texts are designed to transmit the fullness of the unique event of Jesus in such a way that he may establish his reign in the hearts of those who receive him with faith. But the New Testament also attests to an upward movement that takes us back to the Infinite, to what surpasses all knowledge and understanding. This movement is to be found, as we have seen, in the hymn from Colossians (1:15-20). It also occurs twice in the doctrinal section of the letter to the Ephesians (chaps. 1–3), where the ascending movement is carried aloft by prayer (1:17-21 and 3:17-19). We can also include the little catechesis on prayer in Philippians 4:6-7, with its ascending movement.

As far as I am aware, interreligious dialogue between Jews and Christians has not given much attention to this line of research. Perhaps these two spiritual spaces are still too far removed from one another. For instance, we cannot discount the possibility that in the brilliant tractate *Zohar*, Kabbalistic Adamology was formulated by scholars who had a comprehensive understanding of the Christian tradition and wanted to respond to certain christological and trinitarian doctrinal formulations. Today both parties are able to recognize that historical fact objectively.[18] We find ourselves here at the beginning of new and still unexplored paths of interreligious dialogue.

In the final period of the religious history of Judaism, Jesus space encountered a particularly interesting figure in the person of the Hassidic master Rabbi Nahman of Bratslav (1772–1810). Pierre Lenhard, a member of the Congregation of the Religious of Our Lady of Sion, has, on several occasions, called my attention to the striking similarities between this unique Hassidic master, who is regarded with suspicion by Hassidim outside the narrow circle of his followers, and Jesus of Nazareth. If anyone is still in doubt about the Jewishness of Jesus, he should simply reread the gospels and then read the life of Rabbi Nahman.[19] Like Jesus, he too attracted disciples (after a trip to the Holy Land),

---

[18] As is the case with Charles Mopsik in the introduction to the third part of the French translation of the Zohar: *Le Zohar*, vol. III (Lagrasse: Verdier, 1990), 11–19.

[19] Arthur Green, *Tormented Master: The Life and Spiritual Quest of Rabbi Nahman of Bratslav*. Jewish Lights Classic Reprint (Woodstock, VT: Jewish Lights Publishing, 1992). See also Elie Wiesel, *Célébration hassidique: Portraits et légendes* (Paris: Seuil, 1972), 175–206.

trained them in seclusion, and then died at a rather young age. He also expressed himself in exceptionally beautiful parables, which are today considered classics of Jewish literature.[20] He also taught that one is to pray in the greatest possible solitude (*hitbodedut*). Even more, he prescribed that one should speak out loud to God every day for one hour. He was believed to be "the soul of the people" and the *tsaddiq ha-dor*, "the just one of his generation," the only person capable of curing the evils of the world of his time. Indeed, considering that he died so young, the depth of wisdom revealed in his proverbs and teachings is quite amazing. The passion of his love for God in all things, the rejection he experienced from many of his contemporaries, and the close bond he formed with his disciples make him a fascinating enigma, not all that different from the enigmas that surface when one researches the life of Jesus. The space in which we invoke the name of Jesus with faith and the space in which the disciples of Rabbi Nahman continue to witness to their master today are not opposed to one another—two different universes hopelessly separated. On the contrary, the two spaces attract each other, and for us Christians, the story of Rabbi Nahman is a great help in understanding our origins with more precision and depth.

Jesus is truly a Jew—more than we would imagine—and when it comes to marking the anniversary of his birth, we Christians are more Jewish than we realize. In Judaism boys celebrate becoming a year older on the anniversary of their circumcision rather than on their birthday. On the first of January, eight days after the birth of Jesus, we continue to read the gospel of his circumcision and of his being given a name. Following good Jewish custom, then, the New Year does not begin on the day of Jesus' birth but eight days later.

---

[20] Rabbi Nahman has even been called "the greatest story-teller of the Jewish people." Cited by Louis I. Newman in his introduction to *Hasidic Anthology: Tales and Teachings of the Hasidim* (New York: Scribner, 1934), xvii. For an English translation of his parables, see *Nahman of Bratslav: The Tales* (Mahwah, NJ: Paulist Press, 1978).

Jesus speaks the language of his contemporaries, even when he believes he has to distance himself from some of their traditions or practices. In order to say what is new, we sometimes find it indispensable to revert to an older way of speaking. The story of Jesus is one of continuity in discontinuity. Today there is no need to flaunt our differences with rabbinic Judaism for apologetic or polemic reasons. If we opt in favor of a fundamentally dialogic attitude, our differences will enrich both of us, without either one having to worry about being rejected or reclaimed by the other.

In a final rereading of the Jewish tradition, as it has come down to us in three movements since the destruction of the temple, we have seen that "Jesus space" can be quite compatible with Talmudic, Kabbalistic, and Hassidic space. The way is open for mutual enrichment. As we listen to how the other has thought and meditated about messianic expectation over the centuries, we have perhaps learned something about ourselves. More precisely, we may have learned something about the richness as well as the problems inherent in *each* of the ways of identifying the messiah that have arisen over the course of history. The way of encounter we have discovered here may serve as a model for encountering other religious traditions that, historically and culturally, can never be as close to our own as is Judaism.

Let us now set out to meet our other brother, also a son and coheir of Abraham: the Muslim.

2

Jesus and Islam

Of all men, I am the one who is closest to the son of Mary.
The prophets are children of the same father and different mothers.
Between Jesus (Isa) and me there is no prophet.
—"Hadith" of Muhammad according to al-Boukhari (d. 870)

Mohammed is the seal of the prophets;
Jesus is the seal of the saints.
—Ibn ᶜArabi

Perhaps the first thing that surprises a Christian who becomes acquainted with Muslims is that they have such a high regard for Jesus. They know and love "Isa/Jesus, the son of Maryam/Mary." They also love his mother and have no problem accepting his virgin birth. Nor do they have any problem believing in his resurrection and his return at the Last Judgment. The respect Muslims have for Jesus is sincere and fervent. For many Christians this comes as a surprise—even more, as a revelation. It shows that Jesus does not belong to us alone. He is also alive outside the boundaries of the historic Christian churches.[1]

---

[1] Friedrich-Wilhelm Marquart begins his systematic treatment of Christology with an extensive overview of the way Jesus is regarded by Jews,

Asymmetry

On the other hand, we Christians have to recognize how different our attitude is vis-à-vis Muhammad. The asymmetry is striking.

In one of his books Harvey Cox recounts the visit of a certain "Fatima," a pseudonym for a young Muslim student who was applying to codirect a seminar on "Jesus and the Moral Life." She seemed to fulfill all the prerequisites. It was only at the end of their conversation that she told him she was Muslim and wondered if this would be an impediment. Taken aback by this revelation, Professor Cox questioned her further. She replied that she and her fellow Muslims loved Jesus. Unfortunately, she said, the reverse was not true of Christians. They always presented Muhammad in the "worst possible light." Among other examples, she referred to Dante's *Divine Comedy*. That evening Professor Cox looked again at Dante's masterpiece and found Muhammad in one of the lowest circles of hell, the circle specifically reserved for those who had sinned by being a *seminator di scandalo e di scisma* (a sower of scandal and schism). Cox describes Dante's account as follows: "As a schismatic, Muhammad's fitting punishment is to be eternally chopped in half from his chin to his anus, spilling entrails and excrement at the door of Satan's stronghold. His loyal disciple Ali, whose sins of division were presumably on a lesser scale, is sliced only 'from

---

Muslims, Buddhists, Hindus, etc. *Das christliche Bekenntnis zu Jesus, dem Juden: Eine Christologie*, vol. 1 (Gütersloh, 1990), 11–105. He insists that Jesus does not belong exclusively to us Christians, and therefore we cannot keep him locked up, as it were. We too experience him as someone who approaches us from the outside, someone who calls to us, who questions us. In much the same way, Joseph Doré, in his highly regarded collection entitled *Jésus et Jésus Christ*, considers what atheists have to say about Jesus and what Jesus might mean for them—and for us. One of the volumes in this collection is *Jésus, fils de Marie, prophète de l'Islam* by Roger Arnaldez (Paris: Desclée, 1995). In it he comments on all the passages in the Qurʾan that refer to Jesus, explaining them in the light of more ancient and authoritative Muslim commentaries, which are not well known outside Islam.

forelock to chin.'" Cox then adds, "Nothing much has changed in the 600 years since."[2]

A New Age

It was not until the Second Vatican Council that the Catholic Church issued an official text that spoke positively of Islam, devoting the whole of paragraph three of *Nostra Aetate* to it.[3] The first part is descriptive; the second is exhortatory, and it is addressed to "all." The complete statement reads as follows:

> The Church regards with esteem also the Moslems. They adore the one God, living and subsisting in Himself; merciful and all-powerful, the Creator of heaven and earth, who has spoken to men; they take pains to submit wholeheartedly to even His inscrutable decrees, just as Abraham, with whom the faith of Islam takes pleasure in linking itself, submitted to God. Though they do not acknowledge Jesus as God, they revere Him as a prophet. They also honor Mary, His virgin Mother; at times they even call on her with devotion. In addition, they await the day of judgment when God will render their deserts to all those who have been raised up from the dead. Finally, they value the moral life and worship God especially through prayer, alms-giving and fasting.

> Since in the course of centuries not a few quarrels and hostilities have arisen between Christians and Moslems, this sacred synod urges all to forget the past and to work sincerely for mutual understanding and to preserve as well as to promote together

[2] Harvey Cox, *Many Mansions: A Christian's Encounter with Other Faiths* (Boston: Beacon Press Books, 1988, 1992), 22–23.

[3] One sentence of the apostolic constitution on the church (*Lumen Gentium*, 16) also mentions the Muslims (after the Jews): "But the plan of salvation also includes those who acknowledge the Creator. In the first place amongst these there are the Mohamedans [*sic*], who, professing to hold the faith of Abraham, along with us adore the one and merciful God, who on the last day will judge mankind."

for the benefit of all mankind social justice and moral welfare, as well as peace and freedom.[4]

Given the fact that the collective memory of Christians was fundamentally negative in its view of Islam, this is indeed a remarkable statement. However, we need to recognize that it will take more than a few decades to correct ways of thinking that were developed over thirteen centuries. There is work to be done! The work of Christians in Western Europe and the Americas, who are mainly acquainted with some Muslims from the Middle East or Turkey or North Africa, will be quite different from that of Christians who live in those parts of the world where Muslims are in the majority.

The Trappist monks of Tibhirine in Algeria, with their prior Christian de Chergé, have given witness to the cost of drawing close to others with respect and openness.[5] Frère Christian recognized the intensity of his resistance to a deeper study of the religion of Islam. In like manner, a couple of generations earlier Charles de Foucauld spoke of how difficult it was for a Christian

---

[4] *Nostra Aetate*, along with all the other documents of the Second Vatican Council, is available on the Vatican web site: http://www.vatican.va/phome _en.htm. Click on "Resource Library" (accessed November 24, 2008).

[5] Numerous works have described their witness, among them: Bruno Chenu, *Sept vies pour Dieu et l'Algérie* (Paris: Bayard/Centurion, 1996); Bernardo Olivera, OCSO, *How Far to Follow? The Martyrs of Atlas* (Kalamazoo, MI: Cistercian Publications, 1997); Robert Masson, *Tibhirine: Les Veilleurs de l'Atlas* (Paris: Cerf, 1997); Mireille Deteil, *Les Martyrs de Tibhirine* (Paris: Brepols, 1996); John Kiser, *The Monks of Tibhirine: Faith, Love, and Terror in Algeria* (New York: St. Martin's Press, 2002); Christian Salenson, *Pregare nella tempesta: La testimonianza di frère Christian de Chergé, priore di Tibhirine* (Bose: Edizioni Qiqajon, 2008). Some of the writings of the monks themselves have appeared in print, notably two books by Christian de Chergé: *Invincible espérence* (Paris: Bayard Éditions, 1997) and *Dieu pour tout jour: Chapitres de Père Christian de Chergé à la communauté de Tibhirine* (1986–1996). Les Cahiers de Tibhirine 1 (Abbaye Notre-Dame d'Aiguebelle, 2004), and one by Frère Christophe: *AIME jusqu'au bout du feu* (Annency: Éditions Monte Christo, 1997).

to maintain a positive relationship with the Muslim tradition. He was much more attracted by the animistic religion of the Tuareg tribes than by the religious sentiments and practices of the Muslims, even though they, along with Christians, claim Abraham as their spiritual father. He went so far as to try to protect the Tuaregs from the influence of Islam. The council fathers, especially those from Africa who were facing the southward expansion of Islam, were hesitant about ratifying paragraph three of *Nostra Aetate*, especially its final exhortation.[6] To be able to look on Islam with respect and without prejudice will take time.

A Difficult Theological Heritage

A community of nuns recently invited me to introduce them to the Qurʾan. My experience is a good illustration of the impasse that faces us at the present and that will probably be with us for a long time to come.

I began by pointing out some features of this Book—its structure and arrangement in 114 chapters or *suras*, its style, and the different literary genres it contains. I also referred to some of its thematic threads. I then compared the Qurʾan to the Bible in order to show that the Qurʾan's uniqueness consisted in its greater homogeneity, since it was written by one person rather than by a number of different authors and redactors, as is the case for almost every major book in the Hebrew Bible as well as, to some degree at least, for the four gospels.[7] I also situated

---

[6] In *Vatican II. Les relations de l'Église avec les religions non chrétiens, Déclaration "Nostra Aetate."* Unam Sanctam 61 (Paris, 1966), 230–31, R. Caspar comments on the 189 *non placet* votes on the passage dealing with Islam.

[7] The Bible and the Qurʾan are considered by the two religions as the "Word of God." Nonetheless, the significance of these two "holy books" is quite different within the two traditions, as is the way each tradition looks at the book of the other. In order for dialogue to be constructive, these differences have to be understood. R. Caspar, a Missionary of Africa active in Tunisia, has written a very helpful article on Islam's understanding of the

the figure of Jesus in the overall setting of Qurʾanic prophecy. Jesus is one of the twenty-eight prophets, beginning with Adam, who are expressly recognized in the Qurʾan. He is mentioned in fifteen *suras,* and he appears in ninety-three of the Quʾan's 6,200 verses (*ayat*). The Qurʾan refers to him as the Messiah, the son of Mary, the servant, and a prophet sent by God. On two occasions he is even called a "word of God."[8]

Overall I recommended that we turn to the Qurʾan regularly to familiarize ourselves with its images, its names for God ("the most beautiful names belong to God"), its prayers, its literary forms, and the beginnings of a mystical tradition. It is good to do this, I said, especially during the month of Ramadan, when Muslims not only fast but strive to go through the entire Qurʾan by reading six to eight pages of it each day. One-fifth of humanity lives by this revelation. If we want to be citizens of the world, should we not try to understand something of the tradition of the other, doing so without any ulterior motives?

The Lasting Effect of Ancient Hostilities

After my lecture there was time for questions—and I did not have long to wait! In less than three minutes they posed all the classic objections—and clearly implied what the appropriate

---

Bible: "La Bible comme Parole de Dieu: Questions à partir d'un point de vue islamique," *Bulletin Dei Verbum* (Stuttgart) 48/49 (1998): 27–30. See also the short classic work of Jacques Jomier, OP, *The Bible and the Qurʾan* (Fort Collins, CO: Ignatius Press, 2002); and also his *Un chrétien lit le Coran* (Paris: Cerf, 1984), which appeared in the series *Cahiers Évangile*, no. 48.

[8] According to some reckonings, Moses is cited 136 times, Abraham 69 times, Noah 43 times, and Jesus 35 times. The name of Muhammad only appears four times, but the entire message is directly addressed to him through an intermediary, Gabriel. See Geoffrey Parrinder, *Jesus in the Qurʾan* (Oxford: Oneworld Publications, 1995); Georges Chehata Anawati, "Isâ," in *Encyclopédie de l'Islam*, vol. IV, 85–90; Roger Arnaldez, *Jésus fils de Marie, prophète de l'Islam* (Paris: Desclée, 1980); Emilio Piatti, *Islam . . . vreemd?* (Averbode-Baarn, 1996), 112–21, 148–56; French translation: *Islam: étrange?* (Paris: Cerf, 2000).

responses should be. Why should Christians have to read the Qurʾan? After all, don't Muslims say that Jesus was only a prophet? Do you mean to imply that some revelation was given after the time of Jesus? Etc., etc.

I was so taken aback that I found it impossible to respond. The prioress suggested a second conference in which I would be able to answer all their questions. We set a date, and this is how the exchange unfolded.

Why should Christians have to read the Qurʾan? After all these centuries—thirteen in all!—Christians have formulated their response to the Qurʾan, a response that is complete and definitive! All we need to do is recall our rich Byzantine Christology that dates back to the fifth century and was given the following dogmatic and doxological formulation: "We believe in one Lord, Jesus Christ, the only Son of God, eternally begotten of the Father, God from God, Light from Light, true God from true God, begotten, not made, one in Being with the Father." If some people say something different about Jesus, they are mistaken, and we need to correct them. If we do not, how can we say that we are engaging in honest dialogue? We cannot bracket our faith . . . And furthermore, aren't we running the risk of heresy? Both Scripture and tradition teach us that revelation ended after the death of the last apostle. Jesus is the fulfillment of all that has been promised. After him it is simply impossible for anyone to come forth with a new or a different revelation. There is no one else to wait for but the Son of Man who will return in glory on the last day. Jesus himself referred to all others as "false prophets" and warned us not to be taken in by them.

Some will undoubtedly be reassured by the use of such a defense. It appears reasonable and corresponds to the apologetic theology developed by our ancestors. It is systematic, sounds coherent, and appeals to logic.[9] But it also leads to a certain

---

[9] I realized how relevant this position still is when I recently reread a well-known text by the Catholic theologian and now bishop Guy Harpigny: "Islam aux yeux de la théologie catholique," in *Aspects de la foi de l'Islam* (Brussels: Publications des facultés universitaires Saint-Louis, no. 36, 1985),

smugness. Strictly speaking, it tells us that we have nothing to learn from anyone else. All we can do is offer them our way of looking at things so that those who are trying to find their way can make progress in the true faith and come to share sooner or later in the fullness that is ours.

But how do you suppose things look from the other side? What do Muslims think about us? How disposed are we to listen to their point of view and appreciate its logic? Do we not have to admit that their position might even be stronger than ours when they tell us: "We have the final revelation, that which God gave to Muhammad, 'the seal of the prophets,' after the revelation made to Jesus (Isa). In the Qurʾan we find the fullness of revelation. It begins with Adam, the first prophet, continues with Noah, and then with Abraham, prophet and friend of God, the faithful and exemplary Muslim. We also recognize Jesus and his Gospel (*Indjîl*), and we hold him in the highest regard. We have the authentic version of his teaching, because we have received it directly from heaven, whereas you have it in multiple and contradictory forms. The very fact that you have four gospels is proof that this is a work of human hands and therefore must be regarded with suspicion. We really do accept Jesus and Mary, his mother; we affirm his virgin birth and believe in his miracles, his prophetic witness, his resurrection, and his return at the Final Judgment.[10] He is a prophet; indeed he is one of the six great

---

199–239. He approaches Islam as a dogmatic theologian from the point of view of fundamental theology. His exposition is clear and his opposing positions strongly expressed, leaving little room for dialogue. He himself recognizes this in his epilogue: "We should not take our leave saying that nothing else can be said. *That would be to give too much importance to theological discourse.*"

[10] The Qurʾan does not mention the death of Jesus on the cross; in fact, is expressly denied (see 4,157). Someone else was crucified in the place of Jesus, as certain Christians, basing themselves on a passage in the Gospel of Mark, had already claimed some centuries earlier. In fact, one can understand Mark 15:21-22 to mean that Simon of Cyrene not only carried the cross of Jesus but was also led to Golgotha and crucified there. This reading of the text was already known by Irenaeus of Lyons (*Adv. Haer*, I, 24, 4). It is

prophets (Adam, Noah, Abraham, Moses, Jesus, and Muhammad), but we hold to a strict monotheism. 'There is no other God but God.' Any form of tritheism—or 'trinity' as you put it—is for us an abomination, as is speaking of God as 'father,' 'mother,' or 'son.' To affirm any kind of pluralism in God is idolatry, and all the prophets wanted humankind to be free of idolatry. But you did not listen to them. Instead you transmitted a falsified message. We are receptive to the revelation made to Moses through the Law, the *Taurah*, as well as that made to Jesus through his Gospel. In fact, we affirm the *unique* message communicated by *all* the prophets and all the others sent by God, each one of them addressing himself to his own people. The Qur'an contains the Torah and the Gospel. Moses spoke of another prophet who was to come, and Jesus himself spoke of one who would come after him, the *Paraklētos*, or more exactly, the *Periklytos*, the 'man of renown,' which in Arabic is translated *Ahmed*. Now Muhammad is precisely this *Ahmed* who was foretold. He brought to fulfillment the prophecy made by Moses and Jesus."

What is especially striking about the positions of Christians and Muslims is that, taken separately, both of them are compelling. At the same time, some of their arguments can be used to oppose their own positions. Muslims say to Christians, "We have come last; we possess the fullness of revelation." But Christians say the same thing in regard to the Jewish tradition! Our strongest card when arguing with Jews becomes our weakest when we engage with Muslims. In the same way, the accusation about handing on an altered version of the Scriptures is not only used by Muslims against Christians and Jews. For centuries Jews and Christians have used the same argument against one another when speaking about their respective canons. What is especially troubling, however, is that these well constructed arguments seem to do little more than prepare the way for new and violent confrontations, a new crusade or a new "holy war"—a *jihad*.

---

impossible for Muslims—so they explain—to believe that God would have allowed his messenger to undergo the scandalous death of crucifixion.

Setting Out Anew from Jesus Space

Today I believe we need to look for a new starting point, one that will bring us closer to one another as we journey together. "The time is fulfilled" (Mark 1:15).

We can begin by listening carefully to what the systematic and mystical developments of the other tradition have to say to us. This takes time, patience, study, and discipline. Moreover, every step that we take into the tradition of the other will have to be matched by a further step into our own. If we do not become more familiar with and committed to our own tradition, we will find ourselves lost in less time than it takes to tell.

With regard to Jesus, why not begin with the concept of *Jesus space*? This "space" offers us a horizon that is spiritual, creative, and full of meaning. But it only exists in the heart of the believer whose faith is vibrant. Jesus space becomes real when the name of Jesus is invoked with faith. It is verified, tested, and also nourished by reading, prayer, and good deeds. Each of the four gospels makes this space present. Everyone who reads the Gospel of Mark attentively and learns to interiorize the text makes spiritual progress and allows Jesus space to become present interiorly. Those who take part in the Eucharist experience the Spirit of Jesus filling their hearts, enabling them to know the freedom of the children of God and to live with gratitude. Those who visit someone who is sick, spend time with a lonely elderly person, write a letter calling for the release of a political prisoner, say a short prayer, or gaze with faith upon an icon, make this Jesus space more real and draw strength and freedom from it without ever exhausting the source.

Living in this space is what makes it possible to move beyond the confrontational impasse that is created when we limit ourselves to dogmatic comparisons or historical reconstructions. Those who start out from "Jesus space" and move from there toward the "Qurʾanic space" inhabited by Jesus (Isa), the son of Mary (Maryam), will be much less inclined to start making comparisons and judgments, or to reject out of hand the world of meaning that belongs to their Muslim brothers and sisters.

In my Christian world I breathe a spiritual air that draws me into a certain space or force field—what St. Paul meant when he spoke of being "in Christ." When I set out to meet the other, I do so with a different way of putting things together, a different synthesis. Their spiritual world is obviously not put together the same way mine is. There are different parameters, other examples, other experiences, all expressed by a different language system. Certain symbols (water, fire, light)[11] and certain practices (chanting, silence, fasting, keeping vigil, invoking the name of God, etc.) seem to constitute a common heritage and allow us points of entry and mutual understanding. Slowly and respectfully I recognize with gratitude the space in which the other lives and breathes. When I enter that space I understand things in a new way, I see them as I had never seen them in my own space. I am captivated by spiritual mysteries, filled with surprise and admiration at the way they express their faith. Further study teaches me how the name of Jesus occupies its own spiritual space within Qur'anic space. All I can do is accept this fact without passing judgment, and I will only be able to do that if I have interiorized and actualized Jesus space before setting out to encounter the other.

I can say that I have come to love Muslims and their Book. A Muslim once offered me an edition of the Qur'an that contained both a translation and a commentary. I was thus able to read and interpret the text according to *their* tradition. Over time I was overcome by enormous respect for their mystical tradition, and even though I did not understand all of it, I became aware of a loftiness and a tender humanity that are not exactly comparable to what our tradition has to offer.[12] The need to

---

[11] See the book of the Qur'anic scholar Denise Masson, *L'eau, le feu, la lumière d'après la Bible, le Coran et les traditions monothéistes* (Paris: Desclée de Brouwer, 1986).

[12] Those who read Martin Lings's book on Sheik Ahmad al-ʿAlawi, *A Soufi Saint of the Twentieth Century* (Cambridge, UK: Islamic Texts Society, 1993), can see for themselves what I am trying to say. Lings's book includes the account of a Western doctor who treated the sheik during the last years of

defend myself, or to incorporate this mystical tradition into my own, making it conform to my categories and models of under-standing, simply disappeared. The worldly practice of defending one's Christian faith by going on the attack—the classic model of apologetics—was something that no longer had any hold on me. I now dared to believe in an encounter without apologetics, either expressed or implicit, while still remembering the dictum of Emmanuel Levinas: in every "logos" there is an element of "apology."

Moreover, I am not very impressed by the attempt to apply the historical-critical method to the Qurʾan in order to show how the biblical narratives that appear in the preaching of Muhammad can be traced back to Jewish, Syrian, or Ethiopian traditions of the seventh century. Such a methodology is simply inadequate. "Jesus" lives in the Qurʾan. He is given a new spiritual space where Allah (God), the prophets, and those sent by God bring believers into existence in a new way. The Jesus space that is living and active in Christian faith and the Qurʾanic space that is living and active in Muslim faith are not, as I see it, opposed to one another. Nor are they one and the same thing. Each is capable of stirring up the other, after the fashion of the holy *emulation* that Paul speaks of in relation to his Jewish broth-ers and sisters who have not accepted the Christian faith (Rom 11:14). Overcome with awe and respect, I remain silent before this space that so fruitfully welcomes the radiance of the name of Jesus into the lives of millions of Muslim believers. If we enter

---

his life. Even though he was an unbeliever, he recognized that his encounter with the sheik had profoundly affected him. He was struck by the sheik's resemblance to traditional portrayals of Jesus. His clothes, so similar, if not identical, to those that Jesus must have worn, the fine white cloth that he wrapped around himself, and finally his bearing—everything served to reinforce this resemblance. Christ, he thought, must have looked like this when he received his disciples in the house of Martha and Mary (see pp. 16–17). This doctor, whose name was Marcel Carret, sees in the other the icon of what is at the heart of his own Christian tradition—a tradition, however, that he had abandoned. That this can happen says much about interreligious dialogue when it is engaged in simply and humbly.

by the door of this silent respect, a rapprochement between our two great religious traditions should be possible.

Reciprocal Immunization

In the relationship among Jews, Christians, and Muslims it is possible to detect a certain "reciprocal immunization." If, in addition to studying the foundational texts of each tradition, we look at the way these three traditions have developed, we come to the following conclusion: over the course of centuries each of our three religions—all of them tracing their origin back to Abraham—seems to have immunized itself against the other two. Each one has developed its identity by following a well-thought-out strategy with regard to the other two communities. This often took place in the following way: by taking into our own system certain elements of the other, we vaccinated ourselves against the other. These elements, duly assimilated, produced antibodies and sheltered us from any possible influence that might come from the other, and with it the ongoing temptation to "become something else." Thanks to this strategy of reciprocal immunization, we have been able to live next to one another for centuries without having suffered the least contamination.

If today we wish to "enter into dialogue"—the central word used by Paul VI in his groundbreaking encyclical *Ecclesiam Suam* (1964)[13]—we have to begin by honestly recognizing the presence of this mechanism of inoculation and do what we can to eliminate it from our midst. Accomplishing this will obviously be a

---

[13] In the encyclical the Latin word for "dialogue" is *colloquium*, which means conversation or exchange. In *Le dialogue interreligieux: Histoire et avenir* (Paris: Cerf, 1997) Jean-Claude Basset returns to the question posed by K. Dokhorn on the first day of the first major international interreligious dialogue following the council, which took place at Ajaltoun, Lebanon, in March 1970: "Of what significance is it that Christians are more interested in dialogue than the other religions?"

long and difficult process. But peace founded on truth demands no less. Here are a few examples to illustrate this touchy point of reciprocal inoculation.

In our Christian milieu there is a tradition of using the words "Law" and "Pharisee" in such a way that we have become incapable of understanding what "love of the Torah" means for a Jew down to the present day. By resorting to caricature we set up a whole system of oppositions: old and new, law and gospel, slavery and freedom, fear and love, justice and mercy, etc. In our preaching we make reference to this opposition repeatedly— sometimes with great conviction—down to the present day.

If we really want to understand the Jewish tradition, we will have to learn once again to appreciate the way Jews themselves give form and content to their faith by relating it to the law, the Sabbath, justice and love, etc. Secondly, we will have to look at our sources with a critical eye to see how they have been transformed over the course of centuries. Serious, painstaking work will be necessary if we are to have true dialogue and a peaceful relationship with rabbinic Judaism.

In our study of messianic thought in Judaism, we saw a new way of thinking arise after the Talmudic period and take shape in the Kabbalah (from the ninth century on). Structured according to the ten names or attributes of God, a system was developed that made use of the images of a ladder, a tree, or even the physiognomy of the first Adam (*Adam Qadmon*) to describe the way that unites heaven and earth. Its powerful Adamology contains a magnificent, albeit *Christless*, cosmic Christology. There is no longer a messianic figure who comes from God and swoops into history in order to perfect it, as traditional messianic expectation would have it. The messiah has become superfluous. History has been dissolved and therefore is irrelevant. Once we focus on the ten "spheres" (*sephirot*) and their interrelationship, interpreting the Torah as well as the cosmos and the entire spiritual life in the light of this system, it appears that there is no longer any need for a messiah. We have been immunized from the *temptation* of looking outside for a messiah. The spiritual quest is now focused on the ascending and descending movement. Our relationship with God begins here and now in a life that is structured and lived vertically. There is no need to peer through the window of history—to look horizontally—to see if one or the other prophet or eschatological messiah might appear.

If there is to be an encounter between Christians and Jews at the present time, Christians will have to be aware of this profound change that took place at the heart of the Jewish tradition between the Talmudic period and the Hassidic movements of the eighteenth and succeeding centuries.

Within Islam there is a certain totalitarian, or better, theocratic point of view that Western observers find disconcerting and even offensive. What they do not understand is that from the very beginning Islam organized itself in this way in order to challenge the position of Byzantine Christianity in the Semitic world. Some historians are of the opinion that the movement sparked by Muhammad could have been, in the beginning, one more expression of seventh-century Christian monotheism, taking its place alongside the Syrian Church, the Nestorians in Mesopotamia, or the church in Ethiopia.[14] But many contemporary—and especially political—factors intervened to prevent this from happening. Over time the relationship with "the people of the Book," that is, with Jews and Christians, became more polarized and more embittered. The historian of civilization Christopher Dawson put it this way: "Mohammed is the Orient's response to Alexander the Great." That may be a bit strong, but it forces one to think. Centuries after the arrival of Hellenism, the Orient was finally able, thanks to Muhammad, to rid itself of this cultural, political, and religious yoke. But as this reaction to Hellenism developed, it morphed into a theocratic system that allowed for no separation between religion and politics—a replica of Western theocracy, whether that be the Hellenism of Alexander

[14] Arend van Leeuwen writes, "The truth is that when Islam was still in the initial stages of its development, there was nothing likely to prevent the new movement from being accepted as a peculiar version of Arabian Christianity." In *Christianity in World History*, cited by Harvey Cox in *Many Mansions* (see n. 2), 26.

or the Byzantine Christianity of Constantinople. Jacques Ellul, a Protestant intellectual from Bordeaux, devotes a whole chapter of his book *La subversion du christianisme*[15] to the influence of Islam. According to him, this influence has been reciprocal. Islam offers us a mirror, and history shows us that at different times and places the West has tried to imitate Islam. He concludes that Islam has, at least to some degree, interiorized the dominance that Western civilization has always dreamed about.

Without the wisdom that comes from knowing our respective histories, true encounter is not possible. It is especially important that we Westerners not blindly repeat the historical pattern of embittering civilizations by dominating them (Alexander the Great, the Byzantines, the Crusades, the colonization of the British and the French, and now a succession of Gulf wars waged by the United States and England). We must learn to recognize and let go of our cultural penchant to control and dominate and instead work together to bring about a "civilization of love based on truth," a "bond of peace" (*ribât es-Salâm*).

The great ecumenical councils of the fourth and fifth centuries refined the church's understanding of Christ and the Trinity in a manner that was eminently suited to *Greek* culture. But the side effect of this development was a progressive distancing of the Greeks from those churches whose thought patterns and speech were *Semitic*. The Semitic churches showed great flexibility in assimilating Greek thought. It was the Syriac Church, for example, that translated the works of most of the Greek thinkers, philosophers, and theologians. In fact, the Arabic renaissance that brought Aristotle and others to the West was based on these Syriac translations of the fourth and fifth centuries! But there was no comparable activity on the part of the Greeks. Even though the New Testament had been open to both the Greek and Semitic worlds, the official theology of the fourth and fifth centuries was dominated by dogmatic questions and definitions that were specific to the Greco-Roman world.

[15] Paris: Seuil, 1984. English translation: *The Subversion of Christianity* (Grand Rapids, MI: Eerdmans, 1986).

There were political components to the church's distancing itself from the Semitic world. Constantinople and the Byzantine Empire dominated the Semitic peoples, and this domination was reflected in the theological debates of the time. Before the Constantinian period the universal church had maintained a remarkable ability to remain in contact with many different cultures: from Mesopotamia, Cappadocia, Greece, Syria, Palestine, Egypt, Rome, North Africa, all the way to Gaul and Spain. Her ability to integrate such diversity began to diminish in the fourth century, and separation from the Semitic branch of the church was one of the factors favoring the development of Islam as a group opposed to Christianity.[16] In this regard, the Roman Catholic Church has taken an extraordinary step forward by establishing full communion with the Nestorian Church, recognizing that what caused the separation in the first place were misunderstandings based on culture and language.

---

[16] Another reading of history is obviously possible. For example, Youakim Moubarac, a renowned Christian scholar of Islam, who is cited with approval by Guy Harpigny, explains matters this way: In the beginning of the seventh century "Islam cut Christianity off from its Semitic roots and from the Holy Land. It emasculated [Egypt] and completely destroyed [North Africa] primitive African Christianity, while isolating Ethiopia. It neutralized the Eastern Church connected to Byzantium, leaving it nowhere to go but to the Slavic peoples. For all extents and purposes it reduced Catholicism to its Latin branch and thus contributed to the breakup brought about by the Reformation. Having stopped or greatly hampered the Church's missionary expansion toward Central Asia and the Far East, and having limited the mission of the Eastern Church to Russia, Islam made the entire missionary activity of the Church dependent on its Latin and then Anglo-Saxon branch, and that activity was directed toward the Americas. Right from the beginning, Islam cut Christianity off from the great populations of Africa and Asia. Islam can therefore be considered the greatest affliction in the history of the Church." In "L'Islam. Les questions que le catholicisme se pose à propos de l'Islam," in *Bilan de la théologie du XXᵉ siècle*, vol. I (Tournai-Paris: Casterman, 1970), 398. Cited by Guy Harpigny in "L'Islam aux yeux de la théologie catholique," in *Aspects de la foi de l'Islam* (Brussels: Publications des facultés universitaires de Saint-Louis, no. 36, 1985), 202–3.

The time has come to dare to engage in this kind of critical reinterpretation of history. If we want to make room for new cultural expressions of the Christian faith, we have to avoid the errors of the past. The artful wisdom of being different and yet united is the great challenge the church faces both internally and in dialogue with those who are outside. A serious reflection on history is necessary both for the church's encounter with Islam and for Christian ecumenism. If Christianity is to be shaped by the Bantu culture of Africa, or by Chinese, Japanese, and especially Indian cultures, we will have to broaden the horizon inherited from the councils that took place at a particular time in the history of the church.

Moving Forward One Step at a Time

All that we have seen indicates a long road ahead. That is why it is so important to begin at the base and to begin modestly. Something new under the sun comes into being when two or three persons decide on a concrete action for peace, even though it runs counter to what most people are doing. Is that being naïve? Utopian? Indifferent to all the suffering that has taken place in the past? By no means! It is hope made real in acts of love.

The seven Trappists of Tibhirine are beacons of light for those who are still groping in the dark. They teach us how much we will have to suffer for the sake of dialogue, even to the point of giving our lives.[17] Here are some examples that indicate what is possible.

---

[17] An Islamic scholar of the Catholic University of Louvain (Louvain-la-Neuve) published a systematic critique of their witness in the Lebanese journal *El Safina* (Beirut, 1997). His work indicates just how difficult real encounter will continue to be. Relying on the Qur᾽an and the jurisprudence of the Middle Ages (based on the treatise *On the Status of Monks* of Ibn Taymiyya), the author concludes that the murder of the monks was justifiable and unassailable. His reasoning is based on the fact that the monks

In their meetings with a group of Muslims from the city of Medea who were attracted to mysticism, the brothers of Tibhirine used a special format. They sat in a circle, with Christians and Muslims intermixed. After spending some time in silence, they lit a candle. They then continued to sit in silence, forgoing any discussion or prayer. They simply allowed the countenance of God to shine on them, allowed themselves to be "envisaged" by God, as one of the liturgical hymns put it. By doing this an openness was created that was not the result of any particular human activity, not even one drawn from a religious tradition, however revered. Over time such a spiritual practice can profoundly transform heart and mind, and also change the way we act.[18]

Another practice they did in common was *dhikr*, an Arabic word meaning "remembrance." The practice consisted of remembering, repeating, and meditating on a word from one's own tradition or from that of the other. Each one would hold on to a phrase such as "God is greater," "In your light we see light," "My Lord, I am totally in need of the good you want to send me" (Muhammad's prayer), "I was a stranger and you welcomed me." Six months later they would come together again to share the fruits of their meditation.

For several years now there has been a "house of Abraham" in Genk (Belgian Limburg) that exists for the three great families of Abraham: Jews, Christians, and Muslims. Its purpose is to make it easier for them to get to know one another. They keep track of one another's feast days and sometimes celebrate them together. On other occasions they improvise a common celebration using

---

were not hermits, and therefore had to be engaging in proselytism—exactly what they had been careful to avoid during all the years they were there. He never even considers the possibility of a new and different Christian approach to the other, one that is authentically dialogic.

[18] The fruit of such a practice can surely be seen in the testament written by Christian de Chergé, which he ends by speaking to the one he calls his "last-minute friend." He "envisages" him in the face of God as he offers him his final "Thank you" and "God be with you" (*À-Dieu*).

elements from different festivals. For years now they have had a joint celebration of the feast of St. Francis of Assisi on October 4. They gather on the evening of October 3 for a vigil service, during which they listen to readings taken from the Qur'an and the Bible, as well as to passages taken from the writings of Francis and Yunus Emre, a Turkish Muslim poet who also lived in the thirteenth century. The population of Genk is made up of about seventeen different nationalities, and the Christians of the city belong to five different denominations. Twenty percent of the population is Muslim; most of them are Turks and Moroccans. Many things are possible—often much more than one would have thought at the beginning.[19]

All of us are capable of making modest efforts to get to know something about the other: how they pray, fast, give alms; what is really at the heart of their profession of faith. We can read the Qur'an, especially during the month of Ramadan, and, when we gather for a meeting, include some time to be silent in the presence of God. A friend of mine who is a specialist in comparative religion once said to me that the great gift of Muslims to people of other religions is *prayer*. The more we come to understand and appreciate their ways of praying, the closer we will come to a true meeting of minds and hearts. The Anglican bishop Kenneth Cragg once said at a meeting in Lebanon that Christians need Muslims in order to not forget the absolute transcendence of God. "Let God be God." For his part, Hasan Askari, a Shia Muslim, admitted that he needed the concept of a suffering God to complete his vision of a just God.[20]

---

[19] For some years now the Dutch periodical *Begrip* has provided both information and training materials on the well-developed art of eliminating prejudice and becoming more familiar with one another. For example, it informs us that Muslims are not indifferent to Christmas, the feast of the birth of Jesus. A practice has developed of Muslim and Christian women gathering to celebrate the birth of Jesus/Isa.

[20] See Jean-Claude Basset, *Le Dialogue Interreligieux*, pp. 114–16. I should also call attention to the classic work of Maurice Borrmans, *Guidelines for Dialogue between Christians and Muslims* (Mahwah, NJ: Paulist Press, 1990).

Very often it is possible to come together to tackle issues related to education, health insurance, employment, housing. This happens most easily when different peoples get along well together; it also can happen quite spontaneously in countries where there is a great deal of tension, such as Algeria. Archbishop Henri Tessier of Algiers once said that the Christian church "exists for others." In a Muslim country, Christians, as church, are at the service of the Muslim community. If they open a library, a hospital, or a small school, those who frequent it will all be Muslims. These new signs of hope are stronger than the all-too-frequent instances of age-old hostility and destructive hatred.[21]

In his speech to young Muslims at Casablanca on August 19, 1985, Pope John Paul II made the following statement: "I believe that, today, God invites us *to change our old practices*. We must respect each other, and also we must stimulate each other in good works on the path of God."[22] He concluded his address with a very long and moving prayer that his Muslim audience listened to with respect from start to finish. This is truly a "sign of the times," indicating the degree to which things can change. May "Isa," the son of Maryam, help us to grow closer to one another in holy fear and selfless solidarity.

If we continue to reject one another, we have to admit that we are being unfaithful to our own religious tradition, which says that there is only one true God. We all know that our faith in God cannot be reduced to faith in our tradition, our religion, our cultural community. That is why a true encounter can never threaten our faith *in God*.

---

[21] Since the publication of number 48 of *Heiliging* (1998/2–3), dedicated to the seven monks of Tibhirine, Bishop Henri Tessier has published sermons and letters that serve to make the church in Algeria even more dear to us. See Henri Tessier, *Lettres d'Algérie* (Paris: Bayard-Centurion, 1998).

[22] Vatican web site (http://www.vatican.va/holy_father/john_paul_ii/speeches/1985/august/documents/hf_jp-ii_spe_19850819_giovani-stadio-casablanca_en.html), accessed August 19, 2008.

Chapter **3**

Jesus and Buddhism

When Romano Guardini was writing *The Lord* in the 1930s, he already sensed the need for an encounter between Jesus and the Buddha. As he put it, "Perhaps the Buddha is the last religious genius to whom Christianity will have to justify itself."[1] Today this encounter is a daily occurrence, principally in the West, but also more and more in the East. Buddhism—notably Japanese Zen Buddhism and Tibetan Buddhism—arrived on our shores in successive waves and became part of our world. (Who hasn't seen *The Little Buddha* or still doesn't know who the Dalai Lama is?) For its part, Christianity continues to spread the name of Jesus in the Far East as a sweet aroma of liberation.

---

[1] "There is only one great figure of history who comes close to Jesus, and that is the Buddha. This man represents a great mystery. He possesses a freedom so sublime it's almost superhuman, along with a goodness that is cosmic in its proportions. Perhaps the Buddha is the last religious genius to whom Christianity will have to justify itself. No one has yet appreciated his significance for Christianity." Romano Guardini, *The Lord* (Chicago: Regnery, 1954), 305. In this book, first published in Germany in 1937, Guardini compares Jesus to the Buddha at least five or six times.

The writings of Aloysius Pieris, SJ, are a notable example of this approach to the Christian message. Today these two major religious traditions—worldwide there is one Buddhist for every four Christians—are in regular contact with one another, comparing their practices and systems, meditating together, and sometimes joining together to stand up to a culture that is increasingly materialistic.

Studies on the relationship between Gautama and Jesus (the Buddha and the Christ) are plentiful. In addition to scholarly attempts to reconcile the two systems with one another, there are more creative endeavors, such as the work of Carrine Dunne, who sets up six conversations between Jesus and the Buddha; they always end up agreeing with one another in spite of their significant differences.[2] A good comprehensive overview and synthesis can be found in Michael von Brück and Whalen Lai's *Christianity and Buddhism: A Multicultural History of their Dialogue*.[3] The authors devote a whole chapter to "Jesus Christ and Gautama, the Buddha," another to "God and the Dharma," and a third to "The Sangha and the Church." Through their detailed study of numerous schools and various systems, von Brück and Lai have indicated areas for comparative study and suggested how both parties might productively be challenged. I will base

---

[2] Carrine Dunne, *Buddha and Jesus: Conversations* (Springfield, IL: Templegate, 1978). Some classic works are Gustave Menshings, *Buddha und Christus—ein Vergleich* (Stuttgart: Deutsche Verlags-Anstalt, 1978); John B. Cobb, *Beyond Dialogue: Toward a Mutual Transformation of Christianity and Buddhism* (Minneapolis: Fortress Press, 1982); Hans Küng and Jurgen Moltman, eds., *Christianity among World Religions* (Edinburgh: T&T Clark, 1986); Paul F. Knitter, *No Other Name? A Critical Survey of Christian Attitudes Toward the World Religions* (Maryknoll, NY: Orbis Books, 1985); Donald S. Lopez Jr. and Steven C. Rockefeller, eds., *The Christ and the Bodhisattva* (Albany: State University of New York, 1987); Aloysius Pieris, *Love Meets Wisdom: A Christian Experience of Buddhism* (Maryknoll, NY: Orbis Books, 1988); R. S. Sugirtharajah, ed., *Asian Faces of Jesus* (Maryknoll, NY: Orbis Books, 1993); Odon Vallet, *Jésus et Bouddha: Destins croisés du christianisme et du bouddhisme* (Paris: Albin Michel, 1996).

[3] Maryknoll, NY: Orbis Books, 2001 (German original, 1997).

what follows mainly on my own experience, even though I fully recognize the importance of a systematic treatment of the differences between Christianity and Buddhism.

A Difficult Point of Departure

Entering into dialogue with Buddhism presents quite a different challenge for Christianity than entering into a relationship with Judaism or Islam. Over the course of centuries Christians have immunized themselves to any influence from either Judaism or Islam. When it comes to Buddhism, however, the simple fact is that there has been virtually no contact with the Christian tradition over the past two thousand years. These two religious systems have developed culturally and ideologically in complete isolation from one another and in historical contexts that have nothing in common. Added to this is the fact that Buddhism has shaped several cultures. Although it began in India, it has virtually disappeared there, and we now have to deal with other cultural expressions of Buddhism: Chinese, Korean, Japanese, Vietnamese, Thai, Sri Lankan, and Tibetan. Each time we set out to study "Buddhism," we have to be conscious of the specific kind of Buddhism we are trying to understand. Even in a country like Japan, whose cultural identity is deep and strong, there are nine different schools or "sects" of Buddhism, and up until the present time, at least, there has been very little evidence of inter-Buddhist ecumenism within that country, and even less with Buddhism outside its borders. Even though the Dalai Lama is very well known and respected in the West and receives many expressions of solidarity for his people and for Tibetan Buddhism, the Japanese Buddhists I spoke to gave me the impression that he is not very well known in Japan, nor does he receive much support there.

On the other hand, when Japanese masters come into contact with Christianity and try to understand Christian concepts such as "grace" or "sin," they are confronted with the major divisions within Christianity: Protestant, Catholic, and Orthodox. In the theological system of each of these branches of the Christian tradition these concepts are understood differently and play different roles.

At first sight, it might seem easier to enter into a relationship with Buddhists than with Muslims or Jews. But on closer consideration, it becomes clear that it is very difficult to have genuine contact and a serious meeting of minds. Moreover, Buddhists are not always that enthused about encounter. Since the mid 1960s Christians—not all, it's true[4]—are constantly talking about "dialogue," "encounter," and "hospitality," but on the other side there is a high degree of apprehension and caution, and not all that much knowledge of Christianity, which in the Orient still has about it the whiff of colonial imperialism. It is not uncommon to find a Buddhist master who is very willing to teach Buddhism to others, but who does not really have a good idea of what it might mean to engage in a reciprocal "dialogue." There are many reasons why this is so. One is that we Westerners find it easy to "dialogue" because we put such a high priority on *logos* (word, discourse, reason). Asians are much more hesitant about giving so much importance to the word. They are not at all sure that words—even the most venerable of their texts— are a suitable vehicle for spiritual transmission. A really skillful

---

[4] In Germany the Protestant churches have experienced some difficulty in coming to agreement about the value of interreligious dialogue (see the work of M. von Brück and W. Lai cited above). In the United States the more liberal Protestant churches have done some constructive work in this area, but the more conservative churches will have nothing to do with it. In the Catholic Church the response is mixed. At the highest level (the Vatican), for example, some statements coming from the Pontifical Council for Interreligious Dialogue show a much greater understanding and openness than those coming from the Congregation for the Doctrine of the Faith. Harvey Cox, in his book on Islam cited above, noted already in 1988 that ecumenical theologians and those who engage in interreligious dialogue need to be aware of the risk involved in what they are doing. They may experience a high level of agreement among themselves, but find that they are distancing themselves from ordinary believers, or from the official position of their respective churches.

spiritual teacher is one who teaches in a way that goes beyond words, even ignores them.

Some Milestones in the History of an Encounter

What can we hope for from this rapprochement between East and West? What have I personally learned from my more than thirty years of familiarity with Buddhism? What do I see in the future?

To continue reading and savoring classic texts in order to become familiar with the Buddhist way of thinking and believing is surely a good thing. But an even better entrée to the world of Buddhism is engaging in Buddhist practices and then slowly integrating what one has acquired through experience with what has been learned through study. Rather than offering here a new and comprehensive synthesis of the relationship between Buddhism and Christianity (see the literature cited in the second note), I prefer to describe my own experience, as limited as it may be, by summarizing what I have come to understand—and continue to understand better—through practice.

Little by little Buddhism has become part of my spiritual horizon. When I was in my early twenties, I came across a very useful book written by Hugo Enomiya-Lassalle, a German Jesuit who lived in Japan.[5] He described the teaching on zazen (sitting meditation) he had received from Zen masters in the Soto tradition. His book taught me how to sit straight and yet be relaxed, to pay attention to my breathing, and to concentrate by counting my breaths up to ten and then starting over. I willingly engaged in this practice over the course of the two years I was a philosophy student at Anvers (1966–68). During that time I discovered how much I could increase my concentration by devoting a period of time each day to "thinking about nothing." I discovered that there was no better immediate preparation for taking an exam or speaking in public.

[5] *The Practice of Zen Meditation* (London: Thorsons Publishers, 1993).

Reading Lassalle's book also taught me about that key experiential moment called "enlightenment." The many sections of his book in which he described this experience helped me understand that enlightenment is also part of our philosophical and spiritual literary tradition, as can be seen, for example, in the description of the vision of St. Benedict of Nursia, who saw the whole of creation gathered up into a single ray of light.[6] As I studied Aristotle or *The Life of Moses* by St. Gregory of Nyssa, I came to see that these great thinkers also experienced the "light beyond all light," knew a transparency that enlightened them, enabling them to contemplate the eternal in time, the immortal in the perishable. A little later I read St. Augustine's *Confessions* and was struck by his account of three moments of "enlightenment." The most well known of the three is the one he experienced at Ostia with his mother Monica. As Augustine describes his experience, he also lays out the course to be followed in the spiritual journey. First comes the contemplation of nature outside oneself; then one moves toward one's interior self; and finally one proceeds upward from the interior universe of the self to the One who is above us all, sublime and transcendent.[7] Monastic literature, beginning with the sayings of the Desert Fathers, also contains numerous accounts of true enlightenment. I could not read them without being reminded of early Buddhist stories and short treatises on "satori" and "samadhi."[8]

---

[6] St. Gregory the Great, *Dialogues* II:35.

[7] The best summing up of Augustinian contemplation is to be found in the familiar expression *Deus interior intimo meo, superior summo meo* (Confessions III, 3), "God is closer to me than I am to myself; more exalted than that which is most sublime in me." The whole of Western mysticism moves between these two poles of interiority and humble recognition of absolute sublimity. Bonaventure will attempt to interpret these two movements as one and the same, unwittingly preparing the way, perhaps, for the phenomenon of radical secularization.

[8] One example will suffice. "Abba Lot went to see Abba Joseph and said to him, 'Abba as far as I can I say my little office, I fast a little, I pray and meditate, I live in peace and as far as I can, I purify my thoughts. What else can I do?' Then the old man stood up and stretched his hands towards heaven. His

"Everything is grace"

In 1969 I went to Rome to study theology and there I was introduced to the Urasenke Center, an institution dedicated to the spread of the Japanese tea ceremony (*cha-no-yu*). I often participated in the tea ceremony, conducted and taught by tea master Michiko Nojiri. Her way of life, I thought, was much like that of a nun in the world—but in this case a Japanese *Zen Buddhist nun*. She brought some of the great Zen masters (*roshis*) to Rome to teach and also to conduct sesshins (Buddhist meditation retreats). Being in the presence of these masters and observing both their inner freedom and their attentiveness was a great blessing for me. They radiated a sense of humor and a humanity that was gentle but still robust. On more than one occasion I was deeply moved by these encounters. There was little talking, but there was a kind of playfulness at almost every turn, expressed more often by a gesture than by a word.

Once Suzuki Roshi (a Rinzai monk, now deceased) was received at the Japanese embassy. The setting was quite formal, and while one of the dignitaries was introducing him and recounting his accomplishments (in Italian), he sat there fingering a set of beads, apparently not paying much attention to what was going on. During a break a Japanese woman—a Christian who had lived in Italy for a long time—came up to him and asked him to explain the meaning of the beads he was fingering during the speech. He took a small piece of bread and a glass of wine and said jokingly, "Why do you want to know? Mind your own business." She laughed as she translated his reply for me, and then during a question and answer period that followed the break, she asked him the same question. He replied that he used them like a little child would a toy. When a child has a toy in his hands, he's quiet. "It's my toy," he said. "It helps me keep quiet, helps me focus." Immediately a priest journalist from one of the

---

fingers became like ten lamps of fire and he said to him, 'If you will, you can become all flame.'" *The Sayings of the Desert Fathers*, trans. Benedicta Ward, SLG, revised edition (London & Oxford: Mowbray, 1981), 103.

major Italian weeklies jumped in to ask if there was a mantra that went along with each of the beads. Suzuki Roshi then began a very learned discourse on invoking the name of the Buddha on each of the 108 beads . . . He replied three times to the question about his use of beads, each time saying something completely different. And yet I think he went right to the point every single time. He was a free spirit in the fullest sense of the word.

In addition to the tea ceremony, I also studied archery (*kyu-do*) at the Urasenke Center. I discovered the importance of "right attitude" and of paying attention to the breath that accompanies and shapes the rhythm of each gesture and movement. "Life is impossible," said Rikyu, the tea master of the sixteenth century. "Let us then do something that is possible and do it well. Perhaps that will help us deal with the impossibility of the life that is ours." One example of doing "something possible" is boiling water and pouring it over tea powder in a bowl that one then offers to a guest. The art of the tea ceremony consists in making every gesture as simple and as exact as possible, being faithful to the ritual and yet detached from it, being totally present to what you are doing as if it were the most important thing in the universe.

I have often taken part in the tea ceremony. In its most simple form it does not take more than twenty minutes, but all at once everything becomes very quiet and you enter into a spiritual union with what is right at hand as well as with what is infinitely far away. Attention is everything, and on one occasion I realized the meaning of the short sentence with which George Bernanos ended his book *The Diary of a Country Priest*: "Everything is grace." And in fact, at that place and at that time, everything was grace: each gesture, the flowering branch placed in a small bamboo container to my right, all the different colors, the sound of the tea kettle . . . The fact that I was able to have this spiritual experience in the course of an activity that had no religious meaning or purpose shows the power of ritual when it is performed with care and attention.

It should be pointed out that each gesture is regulated by a minutely prescribed and centuries-old set of rubrics, but the ceremony must be performed as if it were the most natural thing in the world. Each rule contains a secret message that can only be discovered by studying with a tea master. What is demanded above all is that at every moment one's intention is completely one with one's action, with the object at hand, and with the person for whom the tea is being prepared. Learning the tea ceremony is extremely demanding and requires an enormous amount of patience, but when one is finally able to perform an action exactly as it should be performed, and to do so naturally, it is a joy to behold. Grace and effort come together to produce a gesture of sublime beauty.

We should recall that the tea ceremony came into being because of a poor beggar. Rikyu was returning from the imperial palace, feeling tense and discouraged. As he was crossing a wooden bridge, he saw a beggar seated between the pilings making a pot of tea. There was something absolutely perfect in his expression of pure pleasure as he finished drinking his cup. "That's it!" Rikyu exclaimed. "From now on I will try to do something as perfectly as he did!" With that he began sketching out a tea ceremony that paid homage to the simplicity and honesty of that poor beggar by being the antithesis of the complicated ceremonies followed by the aristocrats of the time. That tradition has been handed down, without change, over the past four or five centuries.

Zen, Tao and Gita, Vietnam and Tibet

Ever since I left Rome in 1972 I have continued to read about Buddhism, and on several occasions I have gone back to visit Michiko, who will often tell me about the different roshis she has known. Each time I see her, she graciously and ceremoniously offers me a cup of foamy green tea. After all these years I have come to realize that for my personal well-being I need to return to the world of Zen and the Tao regularly. One year I spent an entire summer pouring over three of the most important collections of Chinese Taoist texts. I have also been intrigued by

Thomas Merton's attraction to Zen and the Tao. When I was a student at Nijmegen (1974–76) I took Étienne Cornélis' course on the Bhagavad Gita. Reading that sacred Sanskrit text opened up for me the world of ancient India, with its paradoxes and great maturity.

When I was in his class Cornélis invited the exiled Vietnamese monk Thich Nhat Hanh to a conference. I thus had a chance to encounter a form of Buddhism different from the Japanese Zen I had first come in contact with. The difference, I found, was itself a revelation. When Buddhism arrives in a new setting, it becomes inculturated as fully as possible. Thich Nhat Hanh spoke to us about the difficulty of passing on the true teaching of Buddhism. "We talk and talk, but does what we are saying really get through? And if it does get though, how does that happen?" He offered a number of examples, drawn from times past and from personal experience: ancient Chinese koans, funny and heartbreaking stories about communication that succeeded and communication that failed, accounts of what happened in his monastery and what he learned from others. True communication—communication of the Light—remains a mystery. I have a strangely vivid memory of that conference and I can still recall many of the examples he gave. He spoke from his heart; everything was transparent and clear. But I was also bowled over by the newness of what he was saying. For me it was an invitation to keep on searching, to make myself more fully aware of the hitherto unknown depths of Buddhist wisdom. Ever since that first encounter I have become an avid reader of his many works.

The interplay between reading and encounters—recently I had my first contact with Tibetan Buddhism thanks to a meeting with a master (a *tulku*) at Mont-Pèlerin near Lausanne—is what keeps me going on this spiritual journey. Sometimes these encounters happen purely by chance and through intermediaries. I run into someone who has just come back from London where the Dalai Lama spoke for three days on passages from the gospels to a group of Christians. And then someone gives me the book containing his teachings and the response to them.[9] And so it is that my interior itinerary is extended.

My Encounter with Zen Buddhism in the Heart of Japan

After having interacted with Buddhism in this way for more than thirty years, I had the opportunity to go to Japan in the fall of 1998 with six other monks and nuns from Western Europe and to become acquainted with Zen monasticism in its native setting.

Everything took place in an environment that was totally Zen. We spent five weeks in six monasteries and temples, and we were able to share the life of young monks in formation, not as spectators but as temporary members of their cohort. It was an experience that one cannot get from books, nor even by taking part in a sesshin directed by a Japanese roshi in Europe.

After only a couple of days I was struck by the way everything fit together in this formation program to form a unified whole: manual labor, the recitation of sutras by heart, morning alms rounds in the streets of Kyoto, hours of sitting perfectly still in the zendo (meditation hall), even the highly ritualized and unbelievably quick consumption of rice and soup at mealtimes! By giving themselves totally to the program and not spending a lot of time thinking about what they were doing, the novices came to possess a high degree of suppleness and dexterity. At the heart of the program was the practice of zazen, sometimes just sitting in the lotus position, sometimes meditating on an enigmatic story (koan) given by the roshi.

This last point is crucial: the master is responsible for monitoring the growth of each of his disciples. He leads them on the path of true freedom, helping them bid farewell to their little "egos" and send them on their way. Since we were short-term

---

[9] Dalai Lama, *The Good Heart: A Buddhist Perspective on the Teachings of Jesus* (Somerville, MA: Wisdom Publications, 1998).

guests, we ourselves did not have regular one-on-one meetings with the master. We were, however, able to converse with him and with one or the other of his disciples, and in this way we got some sense of what took place in these conferences.

In contemporary Japan Zen Buddhism is divided into two major schools (sometimes called sects): Rinzai and Soto. Even though we were able to meet with representatives of both schools, the contacts of the four men in our group were primarily with the Rinzai school.[10] What that means is that we were only able to experience a very small part of Japanese Buddhism, which, as I mentioned above, is made up of nine different branches. So what I am describing here should not be read or interpreted as representative of the whole of Japanese Buddhism. Furthermore, we only stayed in monasteries and temples. Both the Rinzai and Soto schools have universities, and that setting is completely different, as we were able to observe at the end of our stay when we participated in a concluding symposium that included some eminent lay Buddhist scholars. In Rinzai monasteries very little time is devoted to study, reading, or making people aware of the current discussions regarding religions, etc. Everything is directed to bringing the *unsui* (novice) to a personal awakening.

In this process the body—physical involvement—plays an essential role. "All knowledge comes through the body," one master told us. You understand something when you realize it fully with your body. Thus all mental activities are silenced—reflection, discussion, interpretation, evaluation, etc. The sutras—Indian in origin—are generally quite speculative texts, as we observed with the help of an English translation made available

---

[10] There were seven of us in all. The three nuns in the group mainly stayed in Soto monasteries, where they experienced a gentler form of Zen, one that was in some ways more ready for dialogue. Women monks are much less involved in maintaining temples that provide pastoral services. They generally do not marry, and they live in community for their whole lives. For these reasons their way of life comes across as more clearly monastic than what we observed in the monasteries of men, which appear to be mainly training houses for the young.

to us. However, little or no attention is paid to their philosophical background. The novices recited the sutras in Chinese, and most of them did not understand what they were saying. In Rinzai monasteries these sutras are shouted out in rapid-fire recitation. Occasionally the abbot will provide a commentary on the Chinese text, but even so the *unsui* understands very little. He accepts his ignorance of what is being said because what is important for him is the fact that the Buddha himself is speaking to him through these texts. This lack of concern for interpretation and rational understanding shows the strong influence of Shinto on the practice of Buddhism in Japan. In some ways I think Japanese Buddhism is more foreign to us than the Buddhist texts that originated in India. Implicit in those texts is the need to use our minds, and because we come from *Indo*-European stock, we are culturally more disposed to do that.[11]

It's quite different with the Japanese. "We study and understand things through the belly," Sasaki Roshi of Tenryu-ji told us during our first conversation with him. This "belly"—the space between the navel and the coccyx—is the secret dwelling place of concentration, and all one's breathing is to be directed to it. We were taught to draw our breath deep into our stomachs by contracting our abdominal muscles up against the vertebral column

---

[11] There exist great differences among the three cultures (Indian, Chinese, and Japanese) in which these texts are read. While the Indians are highly speculative, the Chinese take this tradition and translate it into lively and harsh debates (see the studies collected in Carine Defoort and Nicolas Standaert, eds., *In gesprek met Mencius* [Kapellen: Uitgeverij Pelckmans; Kampen: Kok Agora, 1998]). The Japanese accept the whole corpus, but for them what ultimately matters is that there be a bodily apprehension of insight. For a cultural-historical study of the transformations Zen has undergone and is undergoing now as it enters the West, see the enlightening article of Pierre-François de Béthune, "Dhyana en Inde, Ch'an en Chine, Zen au Japon et en Occident?" *Voies de l'Orient* (January 1999): 2–16. The writings of Stephen Batchelor, who was formed by both Korean and Tibetan Buddhism, offer some further nuances on the different inculturations of one and the same Buddhism. See *The Awakening of the West: The Encounter of Buddhism and Western Culture* (Berkeley: Parallax Press, 1994).

and to count up to ten breaths—that is, ten exhalations. If one is alone, this counting of exhalations can be done out loud. Because of fear or anxiety or something we may not even be conscious of, we sometimes hold back our exhalation. Exhaling all our breath indicates complete relaxation, total letting go, a gradual death to self. And what about our cares, our many worries, our feelings of anguish, or the simple fact that our very existence is so tenuous? "We swallow them down." That was the answer of Shodo Harada Roshi of Sogen-ji. Do not try to rid yourself of thoughts, do not fight them, do not judge them as good or bad. Simply *swallow* them down. Everything is to be done "in and through the belly."[12]

We passed hours and hours seated in the zendo—much longer than we would have ever thought possible. In the first monastery we stayed at, the evening sitting period began at 4:45 and went until 9:00. And then we left the zendo and sat outside until almost 10:00! But what is time when you enter into real silence? "Here and now!" (*Ima! Koko!* in Japanese) is all that counts. That was the teaching of Dogen Zenji (d. 1253), the great master of Soto Zen, who is also cited by those who belong to the Rinzai school. When all your attention is focused on the "here and now," you are not worried about how long you are going to sit. Pain, cold, drafts (the doors and windows on all four sides were always left wide open)—you certainly do feel them all, but if you are present in the "here and now," they are simply what they are: real but limited, able to be endured, and nothing more.

Was There an Encounter? A Mutual Recognition?

We can ask whether or not there really was an encounter, a dialogue, an exchange. Did Jesus and the Buddha actually make

---

[12] When I returned home, I reread *Zen and the Bible* (Maryknoll, NY: Orbis Books, 2002 [rev. ed.]) by Kakichi Kadowaki, a Japanese Jesuit and disciple of Lassalle. Following the advice given by Dogen, the great thirteenth-century teacher of the Soto sect, he proposes that the texts of the Bible also be read "with the belly."

some contact with one another in the course of this experience? Attempting to answer that question may bring us to a better understanding of what is really involved in interreligious encounter, its limits, but also its still unimagined promise.

Did an encounter take place? Yes and no. Or rather, no and yes.

No, because there can only be an encounter when two parties know what it is they are meeting about. However, it was clear that the novices in several of the monasteries had no idea why we were there. At tea time, which appeared to be a kind of recreation period, no one showed the least interest in finding out why we had joined them.

No, because there can only be an encounter when we already know something about one another. But how could a novice, or even an abbot/roshi, acquire a general understanding of Christianity, to say nothing of knowing the difference between a Benedictine and a Trappist? An abbot we talked to had never heard the word "eucharist," and seemed to have no idea what we did when we celebrated it. The young monks, who generally only spend one or two years in a monastery,[13] are mainly engaged in solving the koans they have been given by the roshi and meticulously carrying out all the rituals. Any other "problem" would

---

[13] In Japan there are almost no Zen Buddhist monasteries where monks spend their whole lives. In actual fact the monasteries are formation houses—similar to Catholic seminaries—that prepare candidates for the priesthood. They are "training houses," an expression Japanese Zen Buddhists themselves use. Most of the young novices are sons of priests who are in charge of temples. After studying Buddhism for two years at a Soto or Rinzai university, the novices spend two years (sometimes less; rarely more) in a monastery. There they learn all the temple rituals (some of them very complicated), the chants, and the practices of monastic life. When they finish their period of formation they receive a license that allows them to become involved in the pastoral ministry of a temple. Usually they become affiliated with the temple of their father or their uncle. What gives a monastery its stability is the master (roshi), who is a link in the chain of venerated roshis going all the way back to the Buddha himself.

only distract them from their principal goal and therefore was not given the least attention.

No, because the anti-intellectual climate of the monastery (something that dates back only a century and a half) and the insistence on handing on the tradition by means of practice rather than study closed the door right from the beginning to any interest in contemporary questions and concerns.

But the response also has to be "Yes!" Alongside the drawbacks referred to above and the frustration they caused, there were special moments of real contact and fruitful exchange.

Hospitality always involves communication, paying attention to one another and being careful to recognize that what may be very suitable for one person is just barely acceptable for another. Recall the fable of the fox and the stork. They decided to make up and agreed to pay one another a visit. But how was the poor fox going to get his snout into the vase with the long narrow neck offered him by the stork? And what was the poor stork to do when the peace-loving fox offered her a finely prepared chicken dish with the highest recommendation of the chef? (Wasn't that, after all, her cousin she saw on the plate?) Over the course of a couple weeks our guests noticed our shortcomings and accommodated them. Thus it was that in addition to partaking of their soup and rice, we were also able to enjoy dishes prepared to suit our culinary preferences.

And then there were the times we sweat it out together as we chopped wood, or the afternoon when, together with the abbot and the whole community, we planted fourteen pine saplings in a brand-new rock garden, following the ancient Japanese way of doing it. Bathing in groups of three, sleeping in the same dormitory, and rising together to run and wash at the same faucet—those are the kinds of shared activity that create real bonds and lasting friendships. Did you cut yourself at work? Does your back hurt? Did your little meditation bench fall apart? No sooner was the word out than someone appeared with salve or ointment, or a navy veteran came by to fix your bench. Again and again, we were surprised by little acts of kindness. One day, right in the middle of the morning, the abbot had his assistant tell us, "It's time to take your bath! Yes, right now!" No excuse or delay was allowed. We were each given a new bar of soap and a clean towel on a lac- quered red tray. How could anyone refuse an offer like that? We undressed, entered the shower room, and began to soap up. A side door opened, and the novice who showed us in when we arrived at the bathhouse came in and asked, using signs, if he could scrub our backs. That was the first time in fifty-three years that I was given a back massage, complete with a soaping and a rinse. Right after that we lowered ourselves in a pool of steaming hot water (109°F!) . . . An unforgettable experience of intermonastic fraternal charity in which the abbot and the novice each played his part!

Each of us experienced an encounter, those who welcomed us and we who were welcomed. The intensity of these encounters varied; sometimes they were much deeper than we could have imagined or expressed. That was certainly true on those occasions when we sat on cushions around a low table to celebrate a simple Eucharist. Especially moving were the liturgies we celebrated in the monastery of Sogen-ji, where the community mainly consists of non-Japanese monks and nuns from all over the world (Aus- tralians, Americans, French and Germans, one Greek, and . . . a Dutchman from Middelburg, hardly an hour away from where I live!). There were tears in our eyes as we exchanged the peace, and communion brought us closer together than we could put into words . . . In the fifteen years the restored monastery had been in existence, this was the first time a Eucharist had been celebrated there. God alone knows what that act meant for the community in terms of a rapprochement between Jesus and the Buddha, between the Dharma and the Gospel. Almost all those who were present for the Eucharist were baptized Christians who had been practicing zazen for years.

Coming and Going between Jesus Space and Buddha Space

At the beginning, those long hours spent in silent meditation were not without some inner tension. Sitting in the lotus position caused me a good bit of pain, but the real stress came from being told not to think of anything. Over the years I have developed a practice of spending long periods of time in silence. I do this as a Christian, and I follow an established routine. I begin by reciting some psalms, and so at the beginning of my meditation period there are quite a few words. Little by little these words are reduced to a couple verses or even to a single phrase on which I focus all my attention. It can also happen that I will enter into a state of complete silence without any word or thought. Words cease to exist; they are, as it were, burned up by the intensity of the moment. Normally I sit on a small bench, but that does not mean I remain immobile. In the zendo, however, there is to be no movement whatsoever—not a finger, not a lip, not an eyebrow. You are expected to sit for fifty minutes without any physical movement and without thinking of anything. The only instruction you are given is to count your breaths up to five, or up to ten—if you're not distracted by the time you get to three or six. Because if you are, you have to start all over again.

But in the midst of all these difficulties, there were surprises. One day I was overcome by panic at the thought of again having to spend so much time without thinking. Along with a colleague I went to see Kono Taitsu Roshi, the head of the temple of Shofuku-ji in Kobe, where we were staying. We asked him about the importance of the breath, and he offered us a very thorough explanation. He even gave me his staff and asked me to press it against his stomach and feel his muscles contract as he exhaled. Normally, he said, we exhale from the part of our body that is above the stomach, but we need to exhale from the very bottom of our stomach, using our abdominal muscles to accomplish that. We don't have to worry about breathing in; that happens all by itself.

After his excellent instruction, we went back to the zendo, and I felt more encouraged about my ability to sit without thinking of anything. In fact, that afternoon I was able to focus on the here and now. Breaths were counted with regularity, distractions fell away to almost nothing. And then, right in the middle of the letting go that accompanied each exhalation, without intending it or wanting it, the name of Jesus suddenly presented itself to my consciousness. Along with that name a kind of blessing spread out over the zendo, gently embracing everything—the zendo with its twenty or so meditators, the mountain on the side of which the monastery was constructed, the entire bustling city of Kobe, and finally the seaport with all its vessels, their horns responding to the benediction they were receiving with a deep-pitched, sonorous thank you.

I was sitting in silence at my place in this same zendo two or three days later, concentrating on breathing out, aware that the *jiki-jitsu*, the disciplinarian, was making the rounds with his stick. We had just begun the evening meditation period when suddenly he indicated that three of the novices who were sitting next to one another were to receive his "services." Each one got eight blows of the stick, four on each shoulder.[14] I could clearly see what was happening, because it took place right in front of me. The man's feet actually left the ground as he swung, making his blows all the more forceful. He struck one or the other of those three novices several times, coming back to the youngest one—who seemed to me to be a really nice young man—at least four times. Having received a total of thirty-two blows to his shoulders, that novice must have had a hard time figuring out what side to lie on as he went to bed that night.

Suddenly I was seized by an overwhelming feeling of rage. As I tried to explain to myself how and why that happened, this is

---

[14] Striking with a stick—actually, it is more like a paddle—serves at least four purposes. If someone is dozing, the blows wake him up; if someone is experiencing back pain, being struck helps him to renew his dedication; if someone's knees or hip are hurting, the pain he receives from being struck on the shoulder helps him forget about the pain elsewhere in his body; and finally, being struck with a stick can provide an incentive to those who feel they do not have enough strength to achieve enlightenment. The stick is usually spoken of in terms of consolation and enlightenment rather than of punishment or sanction. However, it is also known that certain disciplinarians, especially the younger ones, let other intentions interfere when applying it.

what I came up with. My practice of silence is rooted in Christian teaching and in the biblical worldview that I have interiorized. One of the expressions that is used to characterize that world is "the bowels of mercy" (*rahamim* in Hebrew; *ta splachna* in Greek). In my bowels, in my gut, I share the pain as well as the happiness of those I meet. Christian meditation also draws me down into the belly (*hara, tanden*). But there I come across something completely different from what the Zen meditator looks for and actualizes. When, in the middle of a meditation period, the master cries out "*Tanden!*" he and his disciples understand the belly to be the place where energy is accumulated, that cosmic force the Japanese call *ki*.[15] As the disciplinarian went around belting those poor novices, he hit something in my "biblical bowels" that did not make me very happy. I was so indignant, in fact, that it was all I could do to contain myself. I sensed that this monk was showing a certain degree of hostility, even disdain, toward his younger brothers as he made the rounds of the meditation hall hitting them at will.[16]

At the end of our sojourn we participated in a seminar in which we shared our impressions and asked questions of the ten or so roshis who joined us. When I told them about my experience, I received two responses. One roshi thought that the novice probably deserved more than the thirty-two blows he received. (Everyone had a good laugh at that.) Another told me that if he understood what I was saying, then I still was not

---

[15] For a good description of the meaning of *ki* see Madeleine Kwong Lai-Kuen, "Le souffle du Christ," in *Le Christ chinois*, ed. Benoît Vermander, 151–67 (Paris: Desclée de Brouwer, 1998). The concept of *ki* comes from China, but Japanese Zen monks make frequent reference to it.

[16] The next morning, as I was out gathering wood, I saw two of these reputable sticks (they are called *keisaku*) thrown on a pile of firewood. I noticed that the broader part at the top was split. Someone explained that the two sticks had been damaged the previous evening. I thought to myself that it must be rather unusual for a *jiki-jitsu* to break two *keisaku* in one session. Otherwise I would have found a lot more broken sticks that were now good for nothing but firewood.

practicing zazen very well.[17] I am now beginning to think that both answers were right. One of the novices later related a Zen maxim that says, "That's the wrong answer! Forty blows for you! That's the right answer! Forty blows for you!"

A Western sage once said, "When you're no longer able to think, then you must think some more." This "some more" means "differently." Therefore, having become aware of these contrasting points of view, I would like to pursue this reflection in a different way by considering the anthropological significance of the belly.

Christians and Japanese Buddhists obviously have different points of view regarding that bodily center called the "belly" (*tanden* or *hara*). One of the places Jesus space becomes vibrant is when someone enters into the "bowels of mercy and compassion" and acts accordingly. For example, Jesus said that the Good Samaritan was "moved with pity" (literally, he felt pity in his gut) and therefore hastened to care for the wounded man who was left half dead on the road to Jericho. Buddha space is realized when someone succeeds in directing all his attention to the belly—the *hara* or *tanden*—in order to bring *ki* energy together in that place. It is right there that one must strive to go beyond all duality in order to be fully open to pure consciousness, where subject and object are no longer opposite poles.[18] The

---

[17] No one admitted publicly that sometimes the *keisaku* is applied with too much force, or that a disciplinarian can administer it with the wrong intention. Afterwards some of the older students told me that in fact it had been misused more than once (in both Soto and Rinzai settings), and that there were even some instances when a disciplinarian struck with the handle of the *keisaku* rather than the flat paddle side and injured someone's head or ear.

[18] This well-known Asian monism is anything but turned in on itself. In the West we may be inclined to make Asian monism more rigid than it is in fact. Officially all dualism is rejected. But the tradition of *bhakti* (devotion) in India, Pure Land Buddhism (in Japan especially), and the speculative theology of Shankara explicitly witness to a developed capacity for relationship with the other, and thus to a monism that is in some way transcended. To think of such oppositions in terms of dualism/monism is insufficiently nuanced. Etienne Cornélis provides a balanced treatment in "Les saveurs

anthropological point of reference of the two traditions may be
extremely close to one another, since both are located in the ab-
domen. But we need to recognize how fundamentally different
these two traditions are. What is important, as I see it, is to note
this difference and to treat it with respect. Is not dialogue—and
in this case we are speaking of a dialogue that goes way beyond
words—first and foremost the art of recognizing two distinct
identities in all their specificity, and then bringing the two into
more than a superficial relationship with each other?

To speak of "bowels" in the biblical sense is to highlight an
ethical and religious vulnerability; to refer to the belly (*hara, tanden*)
in the Buddhist sense is to point to an expanding *self-realization*
that knows no limits. In both cases, the little ego is pushed aside;
in fact it even has to die to itself. The art of give-and-take between self-realization and ethical vulnerability may be the new
spiritual journey that the next generation will embark on. This
intermediate open space within the subject may be where Jesus
space and Buddha space will be able to intersect. It is precisely
because we are not dealing with the same experience that we
must pay attention to the differences and to the comings and
goings between the two. Doing so will surely enrich the spiritual
lives of people who are open to other cultures and other religions.
We are being shown a way to a new spiritual awakening.

A Final Conversation with Shodo Harada Roshi

Right before our departure from the monastery of Sogen-ji
(Okayama) we were able to have a final meeting with the master.
Shodo Harada Roshi served us each a bowl of foamy green tea,
and then we asked him whatever questions were on our minds.
I dared to ask him one more time about the tension I felt during
the periods of silent meditation. What was I to do about that?

---

du divin" in *Monothéism et Trinité* (Brussels: Saint-Louis, 1991), 61–75. The
author is sensitive to the dynamism of Asian monism and compares it with
the self-understanding of the Christian.

I was accustomed to meditate on the psalms or on other texts I had memorized, but now I was being told not to think about anything, but just to count my breathing up to ten.

"It is just fine for you to engage in your centuries-old practice," he said. "Keep on doing it. There is more than one way to come to the light." By encouraging us in this way, not presenting zazen as the only way, or as in some ways superior to what we do in the West, he showed his great respect for another tradition.

He went on to say that the method we were being taught by Japanese Zen monks is a gift they want to share. It came to them from China, having passed through Korea. Its ultimate origin, in fact, was in India. The transmission took place over twenty-five centuries. "And so," he went on, "do not underestimate what we are proposing to you. It is something precious that has passed through many cultures over many centuries."

Afterwards, as I reflected on what he had said, I understood that when someone receives a teaching, they become responsible for it; they need to integrate it into their spiritual life. A year after our time in Japan I realized that, concealed in the practice of meditation, we had been offered a little trickle of living water. If we managed to remain faithful to this practice, the water would become a stream, and then a river so wide and deep that the only way to cross it would be by swimming, just as the prophet Ezekiel had once described it (see 47:1-5). I still think that we Westerners need to be on our guard lest we give in to the temptation to underestimate the precious gift the Zen Buddhists so graciously offer us.

Finally, as his third and final point, Harada Roshi described the process of his own practice of meditation. First of all he lets his senses take into account everything around him. He then leaves all these sense impressions behind in order to attend only to his breathing and his self-awareness. "And then you even have to lay aside this self-awareness in order to enter into the great Consciousness—call it, if you want, the *divine* Consciousness," he said, as if translating into our language what it was he wanted to say. "Once you have managed that, you must remain in that great Consciousness twenty-four hours out of every twenty-four hours." There everything is given: great patience, universal compassion, the Light. It is there that we find the root of all religion. Beyond all rites and cultures, beyond all historical influences and adopted forms, all religion is rooted in this unique Consciousness whose breadth and depth are revealed to those who have finally taken the step beyond simple self-awareness. Coming back to my original question, he invited us to persevere on the path we had begun until together we arrive at the point where the matchless great Consciousness reigns.

That conversation was incredibly powerful and I continue to be consumed by his fervor. His very demeanor showed that every word he spoke came from the depths of his own experience. As he developed his ideas, he manifested the state of being he was describing. Even more, as we listened to him, we ourselves partook of this triple consciousness, as if we were being drawn into the light he was giving witness to. In contrast to all the obstacles to communication and interreligious encounter that we had run into, he made it possible for us to have a "spiritual exchange." ("Spiritual Exchange" was in fact the title of our program.) At the same time he opened a discreet but real space for every subsequent exchange.[19]

An Unforgettable Encounter

Was there an encounter? The more I think about all the things that happened, the more my original "no" gives way to a strong

---

[19] With the passage of time, a comparison with Augustine suggests itself more and more. I am especially thinking of the passage where he describes the enlightenment he received when he was with his mother at Ostia (*Confessions* IX). There too Augustine first of all contemplated everything that appeared before his senses: the landscape, the sea, the stars, the whole cosmos. Then they both turned away from all that was outside to go inward, where God is revealed as "closer to me than I am to myself." Finally they transcended this level of consciousness in a symbolic vertical movement in order to attain to supreme Consciousness. Augustine also believed that this incomparable moment should be prolonged in time, in spite of all the difficulties that may stand in the way.

and beautiful "yes." Here is a final example, the ultimate verification, given by a child.

One of the practices of the Zen monk is to go into the city on an alms round. So in groups of five we set out to a number of neighborhoods in Kyoto, our heads covered with big straw hats. The monastery was not in need of these offerings, which were usually quite modest. But begging is a way to make it possible for others to gain merit. As we go through the streets crying out a long "Ooooooo," old people and sometimes young children come running. We stop, greet each one with a deep bow, and open up our alms bag. The people put in what they have prepared: a little money, some rice, an envelope colored with crayons containing an offering from a child. The monk shows them the name of the monastery written on the bag. Then he makes a *gasho* (a bow with hands folded) and takes his leave.

One day an elderly lady was seated in front of her house when I passed by. Next to her was a little child who couldn't have been more than two years old. The woman came up to me and the little boy followed close behind. I stopped chanting "Ooooooooo," and she rummaged through her pockets for a coin to put in my sack. I then showed her the name of the monastery as I was instructed to do. I was about to perform my ritual leave taking when I heard her give an order to the child: "*Gasho!*" Immediately this tiny little man put his two hands together, lowered his eyes, and bowed down before me, mirroring the movement the mendicant monk made as he bowed down before him. The monk continued on his way, making it impossible for the little child to see the tears that were streaming down the face of that bearded man with white skin.

That monk is still asking himself today what exactly happened in that exchange, an exchange that was more moving than any other he had experienced. What was there about my presence that elicited from that little child such a perfect gesture, which in *his* tradition is given to whom? To the patriarchs? To the Buddha, the Enlightened One, the first link in that long religious tradition? Could it be that by entering so fully into that ritual gesture, I became for that child a faithful mediator of the blessing of the patriarchs?

This was an encounter. I have absolutely no doubt about it. And it took place under the sign of a little child. Here, thanks to the ritual, and thanks to the *gasho* of a little child, Jesus and the Buddha silently exchanged the light with one another.

Buddha space and Jesus space are first of all interior spaces that demand of us total commitment to our own religious tradition. Each one has its proper aura. The differences are not played out in the form of a mutual threat. We need to recognize that being faithful to our own tradition means that we do not feel the need to have to occupy another's space—and much less to insist that the other occupy ours. One of the consequences of the practice of hospitality, with its sharing of experiences and customs, may well be that we feel more at home in our own space. Enrichment, stimulation, challenge, cleansing—for one as well as for the other a whole gamut of outcomes can be imagined. Little by little it may happen that we are able to breathe the air of each other's space without having to talk of syncretism or of betraying our own heritage, or even worse, mouthing the tired cliché that it's all the same thing anyway. In fact, what would be taking place would be something new, for the one as well as for the other, something unheard of and unimagined.[20]

At the end of a similar spiritual exchange program that took place in Europe, one of the Japanese roshis said, "What we Buddhists have seen these past weeks as we lived among you Christians reminds me of a Chinese saying: 'If you want to polish a piece of jade to make it even more beautiful, do so with another piece of jade coming from another mountain.'" How happy Romano Guardini would be to observe the coming together of Jesus and the Buddha that is finally happening in our time. They are two pieces of jade rubbing up against one another and making each other more beautiful.

---

[20] Pierre de Béthune, on pages 15–16 of the article cited above (see n. 11), observes that Zen, as it has developed in the West, has become something new: the final goal is to be 100 percent Zen and 100 percent Western, or, for us Christians, 100 percent Christian and 100 percent Zen, rather than a 50/50 hybrid.

* * *

As we come to the end of this exploration of the way Jesus space intersects with Judaism, Islam, and Buddhism, it has become clear that the same space can be understood differently, depending on the person who approaches it. Interreligious hospitality is shaping a vision for the future.[21] As we get to know one another better, we will not have to go on repeating the fable of the fox and the stork. Rather, as the brothers of Tibhirine have taught us, we will regard one another with fewer and fewer preconceptions, our hearts will be made pure by the silent gaze of the One who cannot be named, and our relationship with one another will grow deeper and deeper.[22] The road may still be long, but we know that we cannot go backward. At the same time, we recognize that we can only move forward one step at a time, without haste. It is only at the end of the road that we will find true freedom and simplicity.

---

[21] With regard to interreligious encounter today, the emphasis is on "hospitality" rather than on simple "dialogue." See Pierre-François de Béthune's *By Faith and Hospitality: The Monastic Tradition as a Model for Interreligious Encounter* (Harrisburg, PA: Morehouse Publishing, 2003); and his more recent *L'Hospitalité sacrée entre les religions* (Paris: Albin Michel, 2007), soon to be published in English by Liturgical Press. The Islamic scholar Louis Massignon already developed this idea years ago, and Jacques Keryell edited a posthumous collection of his works on this theme. See Louis Massignon, Jacques Keryell, and René Voillaume, *L'Hospitalité sacrée* (Bruyères-le-Chatel: Nouvelle Cité, 1987).

[22] It is only in depth that distances are shortened. Thus Paul Ricoeur in a televised interview with Hans Küng on April 15, 1996, cited by G. Ringlet, *L'Évangile d'un libre penseur* (Paris: Albin Michel, 2002), 220. The whole paragraph offers food for thought: "If religions are to survive, they will have to respond to a number of different challenges. In the first place, they will have to renounce all power other than that of a defenseless word. Moreover, they will have to put compassion ahead of doctrinal rigidity. Above all—and the hardest of all—they will have to look deeply into their teachings for the 'over and above' that has not yet been put in words but because of which each person can hope to rejoin the others."

One day a Hassidic master found his disciples playing checkers. They were very upset, preferring that he would have found them studying! The master smiled and asked his disciples, "Do you know the rules for checkers?" No one dared reply. "There are only three," he said. "Number one, you can only go forward one square at a time, never two or three at once. Number two, you cannot go backwards. Number three, once you have gotten to the other side, you can move any way you want."

Chapter **4**

Jesus and Unbelief

Does Jesus space also have something to say to today's unbeliever? I have thought a lot about this question recently because of a lecture I heard and conversations I had with one or the other friend who admitted that "the faith" had become ancient history, but that he continued to be intrigued by Jesus. What, then, is the relationship between Jesus space and unbelief?

Unbeliever, Agnostic, Atheist

We belong to a culture that is godless—"a-theist" in the literal sense of the word. We get on a plane and travel around the world, we make up our schedules years in advance, without ever having to involve a hypothetical "God" in our plans, thanks to computers that can exactly calculate the day and the hour. We construct and organize our world as if everything depended on us and our ability to solve problems by using our intelligence. Contemporary men and women, no matter what religious identity they may profess, are, in fact, "practical atheists."

From a theoretical point of view, however, things look a little different. Harsh words about faith as an illusion and peremptory statements about the nonexistence of God have become much less frequent. People refer to themselves as "agnostics" rather than "atheists," meaning that they do not know whether or not God exists. Perhaps God does exist, but any kind of access to the divine is regarded as problematic, and there is a general consensus that it is not possible to be present to or enter into dialogue with God. Proofs for or against the existence of God do not carry much weight today. Whether we are believers or unbelievers, we simply do not bother with them. As Louis Lavelle (d. 1951) put it, "God is not proven; God is experienced." A good five hundred years before Christ, the Buddha identified fourteen questions for which human beings have no answer. Two of them concern God: "Is there a God?" "Is there no God?" "For these two questions," he said, "there can be no conclusive answer."[1] The contemporary Westerner finds it easier to agree with the wisdom of the Buddha than his grandparents would have.

According to the philosopher Gianni Vattimo, the question of God is still an important one in our contemporary Western culture. He says that as a Westerner, he cannot simply go on ignoring "God." The whole history of Western thought is so saturated with his omnipresent name that he has to become attentive to this issue once again. *I Believe that I Believe* is the title of one of his books.[2] He goes on to say that he owes it to himself to think again about the name of God, if for no other reason than to understand the history of Western thought—and by so doing, to understand

---

[1] Raimundo Panikkar, recounting his own religious quest in *Il silenzio di Dio: La risposta del Buddha* (Rome: Borla, 1984)—a translation and complete reworking of his *El silencio del Dios* (Madrid: Gaudiana, 1970)—refers to these fourteen propositions. The structure of his book can serve as a model for the way we should approach the question of God. The author strives to situate himself at the center of a triangle made up of occidental Christian theism, the vision of the Indian world (both Hindu and Buddhist), and contemporary cultural atheism. His intention is not to renounce any of these three poles but to think about all three together.

[2] *Credere di credere* (Milan: Garzanti, 1996). In English: *Belief (Cultural Memory in the Present)*, trans. Luca D'Isanto and David Webb (Stanford: Stanford University Press, 1999).

himself. After so many years in which people simply ignored questions of faith, Vattimo's way of speaking constitutes a typically postmodern reversal of the state of the question.[3]

Erri De Luca, a well-known Italian essayist, recently wrote:

> I cannot say that I am an atheist. The word comes from Greek and is formed by the Greek word for God, *theos*, and *"a,"* the so-called "alpha privative." The atheist is deprived of God, of the tremendous possibility of accepting him, not so much for himself as for others. He is excluded from the way so many people experience life. God is not an experience, cannot be proven. But the life of those who believe, the believing community, that is an experience. The atheist thinks that this experience is an illusion, and thus he deprives himself of a relationship with this large segment of humanity. I am not an atheist. I am someone who does not believe.
>
> Believing something once does not make one a believer. Believers are those who, as indicated by the present tense of the verb, believe by continually renewing their "I believe." They admit doubt and are continually experiencing the oscillating movement between adherence and refusal. Obviously there are days when a believer stumbles and falls back, sometimes a little, sometimes a lot. That is understandable because to be a believer is the most difficult of all human vocations.
>
> I am someone who does not believe. Every morning I get up early and page through my Hebrew Old Testament. It's a matter of stubbornness, but also of intimacy. That is how I learn. Every day I approach the text with an open mind, and, in the company of those quadrangular letters, I walk through the abyss that separates the meaning they conceal from the meaning I am able to make out. And I remain an unbeliever. . . .
>
> I am someone who does not know where to turn, who cannot bring himself to say "You" to the book and its author.[4]

---

[3] See also *After Christianity* (New York: Columbia University Press, 2002); *The Future of Religion* (with Richard Rorty), ed. Santiago Zabala (New York: Columbia University Press, 2005); *After the Death of God* (with John D. Caputo), ed. Jeffrey W. Robbins (New York: Columbia University Press, 2006).

[4] Erri De Luca, *Ora Prima* (Bose: Qiqajon, 1997), 7–8.

I am sure there are many who will recognize themselves in these lines. It is indeed impressive to see with what respect this seeker gets up every morning and tackles that great text for his daily nourishment, doing his best to understand what he is reading apart from any experience of "God."

"Enough faith and enough doubt"

It is not for us believers to determine what significance Jesus and Jesus space might have for nonbelievers. The study I have engaged in has taught me at least one thing: Christians do not have a monopoly on the meaning and richness contained in and radiating out from Jesus space. We have seen how true this is in relation to Islam. When I was in India, I found the same to be true in relation to some of the major branches of contemporary Hinduism. Moreover, since each of us is immersed in a culture from which the living God is simply absent, we have to come to terms with the truth that living this faith in a secular setting will involve real tension. The two cultures—that of the faith and that of unbelief—together have an impact on the world I am a part of. Dialogue with unbelief begins within each believer, at least whenever a believer accepts secular culture as a given. What is important is that I not become schizophrenic vis-à-vis the world of faith and unbelief that I inhabit, or wall up my traditional faith in a ghetto, but that I strive for a true "inculturation" of the faith in a way that is both constructive and critical.

Jesus space does not exist apart from concrete persons who live it out. For this reason, it does not exist apart from given cultures that accept its challenge. Both the form and the content of this book indicate a desire to keep the door open so that what is proper to me may be brought to a respectful encounter with what is different, and even more, so that what is specific to me may accept what is strange and completely other. Once one discovers and lives in Jesus space, one has access to light and liberty; it is a force for good and a gushing wellspring of new life. In it vulnerability and valor are one; the passivity of patient goodness comes together with active generosity and charity. In Jesus space life is distinguished by a childlike simplicity, a deep-seated and ever present joy. It is a life of gratitude and of paradox. The confidence that "All shall be well," as Christ confided to the English mystic Julian of Norwich, ultimately creates in those who live this way an unlimited openness to dialogue.

The dominant culture, with its resources and its limitations, does its best to find meaning and purpose in life, in spite of the fact that death awaits us all. An encounter between this culture and the faith experience of someone who lives in Jesus space does not necessarily have to be apocalyptic or catastrophic. Still, it is quite possible that those who have interiorized Jesus space and live it out in a consistent manner will meet with resistance from those who do not share this faith. When nonbelievers find themselves in the presence of something that is so foreign to them, they may feel uncomfortable, irritated, turned off, and maybe even threatened. In some cases intense feelings of hatred may arise along with a determination to eliminate what they find so offensive. Think of Saul of Tarsus before his encounter on the way to Damascus.

In spite of this risk, I still plead for genuine inculturation by means of constructive and yet judicious integration. In the area of education and teaching, and more broadly, wherever the transmission of values takes place in our society, it is particularly important to search out symbols, a way of thinking, and a language that will bring about an integration of faith and secular culture rather than a division into separate or even hostile camps. In order to be able to do this, we have to rediscover the power of genuine initiation, followed by a "mystagogy" that supports those who have been brought into the faith and enables them to interpret what they have experienced.[5]

---

[5] "Initiation" and "mystagogy" are technical terms that refer to two stages of Christian initiation developed in the first centuries. First of all, one was "initiated," a process that was relatively long and thorough and that involved much more than a simple transmission of doctrine. By way of symbols, stories, and rites, catechumens received a full experience of

Jesus space is a space that glows. Wherever there is an opening, be that in a text, a gospel, a work of art (the *Beau Dieu* of the Amiens cathedral, Grünewald's Crucifixion, or Andrei Rublev's icon of the Trinity), or in the kind of witness given by an individual or community (Mother Teresa of Calcutta, venerated by Hindu swamis; the seven Trappist monks of Tibhirine, honored by Algerian Muslims; Jean Vanier and the L'Arche community), you can expect that someone from another religion or even an unbeliever will be strongly affected. When our humanity is transformed and elevated by its contact with Jesus space, it attracts, challenges, and lifts others to go beyond themselves in an ongoing movement of transformation.

The Voice of Nonbelieving Witnesses

Not too long ago I read the transcript of an interview with Raymond Gérôme, a well-known actor and orator. One of his major theatrical successes was reading the whole of the Gospel of Mark. After each performance there was time for discussion. He himself recounts that one day someone came to see him:

> He was visibly troubled, more so than other visitors who were already quite familiar with what this was all about, who knew, so to speak, the lay of the land. He said, "This is a story I'd never heard before." Someone interrupted him to say that you have to know something in order to be able to appreciate it. He replied, "I don't know if there is a God, so I certainly don't know if there is a Son. I got the whole thing in one fell swoop. But even if this was all made up yesterday, I still think it's a good thing for humanity."

---

the new life to which they were to be admitted. "Mystagogy" was the complementary catechesis given to the newly initiated to teach them how to recognize and interiorize what they had experienced. Today we recognize how essential it is to recover this way of transmitting the faith and then accompanying the newly initiated with mystagogic catechesis.

Raymond Gérôme added, "I really liked that guy. He was extraordinary."[6]

Whether it is historically based or not, the story of Jesus as told by Mark is still "a good thing for humanity."

A similar point of view was expressed in a conversation between Umberto Eco, who admits to having been a believer but is one no longer, and Cardinal Carlo Maria Martini, when he was archbishop of Milan. Eco observes:

> But admit that even if Christ were only a character in a great story, the fact that this story could have been imagined and desired by featherless bipeds who only knew that they didn't know, would be as miraculous (miraculously mysterious) as the fact that the son of a real God was really incarnated. This natural and earthly mystery would never stop stirring and softening the hearts of nonbelievers. [As he put it a bit earlier,] Why are you taking away from the layman the right to avail himself of the example of a forgiving Christ?[7]

I am suddenly reminded of two gospel passages.

At the end of the twelfth chapter of the Gospel of Mark, we see Jesus seated at the temple gate. A poor widow enters the scene and puts two copper coins in the box for offerings. As far as we know, this woman does not believe in Jesus; she has no contact with him, nor he with her. He does not speak to her. Even after she has made her offering, he says nothing to comfort her and assure her that everything will be all right when she returns home. Nothing. In the gospel account all she has is a walk-on role. Jesus exits; she enters. She places some money in the offering box in the very place that Jesus had just condemned as a "den of robbers" (Mark 11:17). Nonetheless, Jesus praises this woman and points out that she has given more than all the others because she has given "all she had to live on" (12:44). He makes her an outstanding example for his disciples and for all the Christian

---

[6] In *La Maison Dieu*, no. 219 (1999): 116.

[7] *Belief or Nonbelief?* trans. Minna Proctor (New York: Arcade Publishing, 2000), 102, 100.

community to follow. In the school of Jesus we learn to appreciate the openness that can be seen in other people as a privileged
revelation of what is offered to us in the gospels. The boundless
generosity of this Jewish widow is a light that illuminates the
world of the gospel. From this it follows: (1) that nonbelievers
can also understand the essential message of Jesus; (2) that they
are therefore very capable of appreciating the openness and the
freedom that shine forth in the gospel; and (3) once again, that
believers need to abandon any sense that they have a monopoly
on understanding the meaning of life that comes to us in such
a striking way through the life of Jesus. In fact, they can learn
something about it from those who do not share their faith.

In the third chapter of Mark's gospel Jesus is caught up in a
debate with theologians. The scribes from Jerusalem interpret
his numerous exorcisms as the work of Beelzebub. In their eyes,
Jesus himself is possessed, and not just by any evil spirits but by
the prince of demons himself. The response of Jesus is enlightening on more than one level. His final words are of special interest
to us here: "Truly I tell you, people will be forgiven for their sins
and whatever blasphemies they utter; but whoever blasphemes
against the Holy Spirit can never have forgiveness, but is guilty
of an eternal sin" (3:28-29).

If someone were to draw near Jesus because he or she was
overcome by his exemplary goodness, his love of enemies, the
power of his forgiveness, but was unable to give full acceptance
to the orthodox faith of the traditional churches, is it conceiv-
able that Jesus would refuse pardon to such a person? The text
is straightforward: this person will receive God's pardon. But
if "the Holy Spirit" in the person of Jesus is explicitly denied—
something that is very rare, something, in fact, that only occurs
among "theologians"—what we then have is a radical refusal
of the very communication through which pardon is offered.
This refusal is taken seriously; human freedom with all its consequences is respected totally. Taking everything into consideration, the conclusion Jesus comes to does not really constitute
a condemnation but is simply the consequence of strict logic.
Those who refuse to recognize the presence of the Holy Spirit in

Jesus withdraw themselves, by that very act, from the one who pardons. Inversely, if there is no opposition to the Spirit, pardon is always possible. Once again we see the inclusive power of the gospel. At the heart of the gospel tradition is the demand that we be open to and respect those who are "not following us" (see Mark 9:38-40: "Whoever is not against us is for us").

Jesus and his radiating space are accessible even to those who say they are nonbelievers. Certain nonbelievers themselves give witness to that. Jesus himself says so very strongly in Mark 3:28-29. Jesus space is real. Wherever it is actualized, human beings are called to be more fully human, in the sense understood by Pascal: "Man infinitely surpasses man." Human beings are continuously being called to go beyond themselves. Who can deny that nonbelievers are also given this vocation?

For all its brevity, our consideration of the relation of the Christian to the nonbeliever is one more indication that the notion of Jesus space provides rich resources for interreligious dialogue.

Epilogue:
In the Space of the Transfigured Jesus

Faith in the risen Christ, expressed in celebration, contemplation, and action, draws us ever more deeply into what I have called "Jesus space" and then summons us to move outward to encounter other great religious traditions: Judaism, Islam, and Buddhism. I have tried to move from one space to another prudently, with reserve and great respect, in order to be more receptive to the rich differences that are present in other traditions and to the revelation they can offer us. I am acutely aware that we are just at the beginning of a new way of relating to other religions. To rediscover who we are as a religious community and together make real the vision of peace in our time requires the humility of the biblical "poor," the *anawim*. Humbly admitting our poverty becomes all the more necessary when our dialogue partner is a nonbeliever or an agnostic.

Jesus space is more than a simple historical memory, and it is larger than the limits and content established by dogmatic formulas. Whoever lives in this space knows light, liberty, humility, and an immeasurable goodness that is radiant and recreative. To those who are firmly grounded in their paschal faith, Jesus space offers a vision of the future, a future that is already at work in us here and now. At the heart of the oldest gospel that has come down to us, Mark offers us a picture of Jesus radiant in glory (9:2-9). We can read it together as a way of bringing this study to a close. The first time through we will pay close attention to the literal meaning of the text. Then we will reread it as it has been interpreted by Russian iconography, specifically by the school of Novgorod toward the end of the fifteenth or the beginning of the sixteenth century.

The mystery of Jesus will reveal itself to our spiritual gaze with much greater clarity and power if we dare to look toward our ultimate destiny. Many of the problems we cannot solve intellectually no longer torment us if we turn our gaze to what is coming toward us from the future. A good number of our existential challenges will be illuminated and transfigured by the conviction that "All shall be well," as Christ assured the English mystic Julian of Norwich. Those who live by the future that ultimately awaits them are surprised to discover that they experience a new confidence and lightness in the most ordinary routines of daily life, even if they are inevitably "mortal." Paul consoles the new community founded at Thessalonica by presenting it with as clear a picture as he can of the future that awaits it. Rabbi Akiva encourages and consoles his colleagues and friends by calling their attention to what God has promised for the future, fully aware that the recent past has been a disaster and that the present, with the temple in ruins, does not offer any way out.[1]

Mark 9:2-9

Six days later, Jesus took with him Peter and James and John,

The initiative belongs to Jesus: he "took with him . . ." The disciples have had a whole week to reflect on his words about a

---

[1] According to an article in the review *Heilging* 45 (1995/1–2): 44–48, both Julian and Rabbi Akiva turn things around completely by looking at reality as God sees it in the future. "Learn to support and to assimilate everything you see not on the basis of what you have seen or thought in the past, but of what God has promised for the future." For an introduction to Rabbi Akiva's way of reading texts, see my article "Les quatre sens de l'Écriture" in *Vie Spirituelle*, no. 715 (May–June 1996): 330 and n. 12 with its reference to Elie Wiesel's *Célébration talmudique: Portraits et légendes* (Paris: Seuil, 1991), 142–63. (*Sages and Dreamers: Biblical, Talmudic, and Hasidic Portraits and Legends* [New York: Summit Books, 1991].)

suffering Messiah who will be rejected and put to death (Mark 8:31). He had also told them about the trials that awaited them. To follow him will mean public condemnation, having to carry their own cross, being ready to give up absolutely everything. If any of them are ashamed of him, of his words, or of the gospel, "the Son of Man will also be ashamed [of them] when he comes in the glory of his Father" (8:34-38). To that Jesus had added, "Truly I tell you, there are some standing here who will not taste death until they see that the kingdom of God has come with power" (9:1). For those who have eyes to see, the future is breaking in here and now, at least on occasion.

"Six days later," Jesus takes the initiative again. He calls only a few, those who will see the reign of God coming with power. He summons them by name, "Peter and James and John," three of the first four who were called, the three who witnessed the raising of the daughter of Jairus, the same three who will be with him during his agony in the Garden of Olives. Among the twelve, these three hold a special place as witnesses. They are known by name and are presented as individuals with distinctive personalities.[2] They are our intermediaries for the unique event that is about to take place. We will be looking at it through their eyes.

. . . and led them up a high mountain apart, by themselves.

The three disciples are remarkably passive. It is almost as if Jesus were carrying them to the mountaintop in his arms or on his shoulders. The elevation, separation, and solitude come together to highlight the exceptional character of what is going to take place. They are separated from the crowds, lifted up and set apart. Having themselves become one, they are now open to the One and dwell in his presence. The setting calls to mind the passage in Exodus (24:10, 16) that describes how Moses, after

---

[2] The medieval mystic Ruysbroek, attending to the etymology of their proper names, identifies three qualities that are indispensable for anyone who wants to participate in the event: Peter (*rock*: firmness of faith); James (*constancy*: resistance to evil); John (*grace* and *love*).

the ratification of the covenant, goes to the top of the mountain with some companions to contemplate the glory of God. One is also reminded of the story of Elijah's solitary sojourn on the top of Mount Horeb (1 Kgs 19).

And he was transfigured before them, and his clothes became dazzling white, such as no one on earth could bleach them.

Now it is Jesus who becomes passive in the extreme. He *is changed*; he *becomes* something else. His metamorphosis (the literal meaning of the Greek verb) fills his whole being with light. Mark suggests this inner transformation by referring to what is on the outside of his body, his clothing. It becomes brilliantly white, whiter than anything one could imagine and therefore not of "this earth." Mark's style is evocative, poetic. He does not say anything about Jesus' body, his face, his eyes. We are reminded of the young Isaiah who recounts how he was able to see the Lord in the temple. "I saw the Lord" is how he vigorously begins the account in the sixth chapter! In order to suggest just how awesome the event was, he says that "the hem of his robe filled the temple" (Isa 6:1-2). The exterior of the exterior of Isaiah's vision of the Lord was already so overwhelming that it filled everything. Having seen the Lord himself, what more could Isaiah possibly say? Mark follows the literary tradition attested to by this chapter of the book of Isaiah.

Luke situates the scene at night and indicates that everything happened while Jesus was praying. Mark tells us that Jesus underwent a transformation, and the passive form of the verb indicates that it was *God* who brought it about. It is because of Jesus' relationship with God that the disciples see the brilliant light that bursts forth from his body. It is clear, though not explicitly stated, that Jesus wants to be seen; he takes his chosen ones with him because he *really wants* to show them something. He allows them to see him like this. Everything has to do with his intimate relationship with God. "[N]o one knows the Son," and "no one knows the Father," unless it be the Son who wishes to show them how he relates to the Father, wishes to reveal to them this mysterious reciprocity within the Godhead (see Matt 11:27). Jesus confides to these three disciples what he holds most dear and most confidential, and in so doing he reveals his great love for them.

And there appeared to them Elijah with Moses, who were talking with Jesus.

The metamorphosis of Jesus becomes larger by including the glorious vision of two others, first Elijah and then Moses. The two converse with Jesus. What do they see, and what do they hear?

This sudden expansion is quite remarkable. A conversation among equals, without any regard for the centuries that separate them from one another, piques our interest. At the very core of his identity Jesus is not remote or solitary; he is in conversation with the greatest figures of history. As we reflect on this scene twenty centuries after it took place, what captures our imagination is the thought that it has become much more inclusive. Today it is not just Elijah and Moses who are in conversation with Jesus but also the Buddha and Socrates, Muhammad and Gandhi, Martin Luther King and Mother Teresa of Calcutta.

Mark says nothing about the specific content of this three-way conversation. Only Luke makes explicit that they "were speaking of his departure, which he was about to accomplish at Jerusalem" (Luke 9:31). They talked about what was essential, about death as fulfillment, a death that was to take place in Jerusalem, Luke's geographical and theological focal point, the city where scriptural messianism is to be accomplished. The conversation continues through the centuries, for the depth of Jesus space is inexhaustible, and the meaning of life and death runs through all literature, all cultures. Life's huge problems do not come to an end with death. When Socrates speaks about death in Hades, he does so in conversation with Minos and Rhadamathe, Hesiod and Homer. He hopes to be able to ask the one and only question that he is ultimately concerned about: "What is virtue? What is it that makes us human?" As his *Apology* makes clear, Socrates was convinced that death does not put an end to such questions.

Then Peter said to Jesus, "Rabbi, it is good for us to be here;
let us make three dwellings, one for you, one for Moses,
and one for Elijah."

In the presence of Moses, master of all masters in Israel, rabbi of all rabbis, Peter addresses Jesus as "Rabbi." He is not just being polite! With this one word he—and through him Mark— testifies to the new and full authority that Christians acknowl- edge in Jesus. Those for whom Peter proposes to make three "dwellings" (tents or huts) are listed in hierarchical order: first Jesus, then Moses, then Elijah. That ordering corresponds to what people of the time were awaiting in the messianic age: first Elijah would appear, and then the prophet of the end of time, the Messiah, the new Moses (see Mal 3:23 and Deut 18:15, 18). This arrangement confirms the christological creed of the evangelist and of the community: Jesus is greater than Elijah, different from Moses, and superior to him as well.

The reason people put up a hut or a tent is to prolong a memo- rable moment in their life, even if it is for only a short time. This was the case, for example, with the custom of ritually erecting tents for the feast of Booths, which lasted for eight days. People want to hold on to the eternal in time, the heavenly on earth, the transhistorical in the present instant. Peter has been deeply affected by this overpowering and ineffable experience, and does his best to hold on to what cannot be grasped. The author of the narrative comments on how completely inadequate his response was.[3]

He did not know what to say, for they were terrified.

Peter thus spoke for all three, for they were all terrified. The Greek work *ekphoboi* is rather rare and is only found in one pas- sage in the Greek translation of the Bible, namely Deuteronomy 9:19, where it is spoken by Moses: "For I was afraid . . ." (see

---

[3] The response of the disciples of Jesus to his agony is also inadequate (see Mark 14:40). The evangelist thus shows us that both the passion and the glory of the Son of Man are completely beyond our comprehension.

Heb 12:21). The choice of this rare word establishes a link between the experience of Moses and that of the disciples. The fathers of the church, noting the verbal connection, interpret this passage to mean that Moses saw the glory of the Son of God.

Father Emmanuel Lanne, a Benedictine monk from Chevetogne, counted up all the words in the Gospel of Mark and discovered that at the very middle of the gospel are the three Greek words *ekphoboi gar egenonto*, "for they were terrified" (9:6). His discovery was remarkable indeed, because it shows that the account of the transfiguration is at the mathematical center of Mark's composition, and that the expression at the very middle of his gospel corresponds exactly to its very last words: "for they [the women] were afraid" (*ephobounto gar*; Mark 16:8). Confronted by the announcement of the resurrection at the tomb and confronted by the transfiguration on the mountain in Galilee, Mark provides only one fitting response: reverential fear. Even if the message is decidedly positive—the same Peter says, "it is good for us to be here" (9:5) and the women hear, "He has been raised . . . he is going ahead of you to Galilee" (16:6, 7)—they are so dazed that their only reaction is one of holy fear. (See Eccl 12:13: "The end of the matter; all has been heard. *Fear God*, and keep his commandments; *for that is the whole duty of everyone*" [italics added].)

Then a cloud overshadowed them,

Peter's proposal to build three tents does not provoke any reaction at first. But then a cloud comes and covers the mountain. Peter wanted to cover the event with a tent, so to speak, just as David once wanted to build a house for the ark of the covenant. But now the disciples themselves are covered over by the shadow of the divine cloud, just as David was when he heard from the mouth of the prophet Nathan: It is not you who will build me a "house"; rather, by giving you offspring, I will build you a "house." From your offspring will come one who will construct a temple for me (see 2 Sam 7:11-13). Anyone who thinks about grasping the Ungraspable by one means or another is immediately and completely grasped himself.

and from the cloud there came a voice,

As was the case at the baptism of Jesus by John at the beginning of the gospel (1:10-11), the cloud and the voice indicate the proximity of God, who comes to bring the event to a close and indicate its meaning. The beginning and the end of the Gospel of Mark, the prologue and the epilogue, are joined together here in two verses (see 16:8 and 9:6; 1:11 and 9:7). This gives even greater significance to the three words of 9:6b (*ekphoboi gar egenonto*). Tradition has spontaneously associated the cloud with the Spirit, and thus Father, Son, and Holy Spirit are all three attested to.

"This is my Son, the Beloved; listen to him!"

For a moment, Peter wanted to take part in the conversation, but with the coming of the cloud the conversation takes another turn. A voice comes out of the cloud; the Father speaks, refers to Jesus as his Son, and in so doing reveals himself as "father." The voice is no longer addressed only to Jesus, as was the case in the prologue ("You are my Son," 1:11), but to the three witnesses. They learn what the reader/hearer—together with Jesus—had learned at the very beginning. The voice confirms what the reader already knows, and it lays upon the reader a final, pressing charge: "[L]isten to him!" The distance between the three disciples and the reader has become extremely small. By listening to this "Beloved" without reserve—the Beloved to whom Moses, Elijah, and all the Scriptures refer—everything will make sense, everything will be fulfilled.

In the one short phrase that the voice speaks from the cloud, we find three quotations from the First Testament, all of them messianic in character:

- *"This is my Son"* comes from Psalm 2:7. The Son of David receives his divine investiture. He becomes a king.

- *"the Beloved"* comes from Genesis 22:2, where Isaac is bound for sacrifice on Mount Moriah. Jesus is the Isaac of God, the son who comes onto the stage of history as the final envoy who, contrary to the first Isaac, will *not* be spared (see Mark 12:6-8; also 8:31, where Jesus teaches his disciples for the first time about the necessity of suffering and about the death of the Son of Man).

- *"[L]isten to him!"* comes from Deuteronomy 18:15, 18, where Moses foretells the coming of "a prophet like me from among your own people" (notice how Jesus speaks about himself in Mark 6:4: "Prophets are not without honor, except in their hometown, and among their own kin, and in their own house"). "[Y]ou shall heed such a prophet," says Moses in Deuteronomy 18. The disciples are now in the presence of the new Moses of the end time. They must listen to and hold on to his words without exception, even when he speaks about his rejection, death, and resurrection, or about the paradoxes inherent in life, when loss is gain, and gain is loss (see 8:31, 34-38). Every question about the identity of Jesus and about the demands of following him find their answer and their definitive solution in this single, key word coming from the cloud. In it Jesus is confirmed as God's official envoy, no matter what may happen to him later. Those who listen to him and are ready to follow him can now depend on the authority of a word that comes from God.

Suddenly when they looked around, they saw no one with them anymore, but only Jesus.

The vision ends; there is nothing more to hear. *They saw no one with them anymore, but only Jesus.* He is all they have from now on, as was the case on the lake when all they had was "one loaf with them in the boat" (see Mark 8:14). Or should we see something more in the narrator's final comment?

Lev Gillet, a monk of the Eastern church, comments on this passage as follows:

> If you look at the sun for too long a time, you run the risk of damaging your retina. If that happens, you will see a black

spot wherever you look. If you have seen the great Light on the mount of the transfiguration, your vision is changed. On coming down from the mountain, no matter where you look, you see the light of the Only Begotten reflected in every being, every face, every person.

As they were coming down the mountain,
he ordered them to tell no one about what they had seen,
until after the Son of Man had risen from the dead.

They will not be able to put into words what they have seen until they have experienced something else: the resurrection of the Son of Man from the dead. What has just happened is connected to Jesus' resurrection—and also to "the kingdom of God [that comes] with power," and "the Son of Man . . . [who] comes in the glory of his Father with the holy angels" (see 9:1 and 8:38, immediately preceding our pericope). What happened anticipates what is to come: Jesus here refers not only to the resurrection of the Son of Man but also to his appearance in glory and power at the end of time.

From the point of view of the reader, however, the resurrection is already past; in fact, some of them were witnesses to it. What is yet to come is his glorious appearance at the end of time. The three disciples who were present at the scene will speak as witnesses later on, after having also seen the corroborating light of Jesus risen from the dead. There is a beauty and fullness, a power and glory that cannot be spoken of except after a purification as radical as that undergone by the Son of Man: "I was dead, and see, I am alive for ever and ever" (see Rev 1:17-18). When one follows Jesus, one's life remains obscure, but it is mysteriously guided and supported by a glimmer of light that is already perceptible. Certain people have already seen this light, and they give witness to it. The light that shone on them widened their field of vision: they saw Jesus in conversation with the greatest figures of revelation history. Their study of the prophetic writings served to confirm this light, which they compared to "a lamp shining in a dark place, until the day dawns and the morning star rises in your hearts" (2 Pet 1:19). A new day has dawned; the morning star shines within our hearts; the light of biblical witnesses accompanies our vigils. We make our way toward an even greater light, knowing all the while that our transformation or transfiguration has already begun through the working of the Holy Spirit, the agent of glory.

The Icon of the Transfiguration

With the text and the commentary of the transfiguration account in our hearts and minds, let us now continue our "reading" by considering an icon that offers us a visual Christology, a light that takes material form. Out of the many icons on the transfiguration of Jesus I have chosen one that comes from the school of Novgorod in the north of Russia at the beginning of the seventeenth century.

My choice is obviously subjective. I have lived with this icon for many years. Experience has taught me that it takes a long time for a Westerner to enter into the spiritual space in which the Eastern iconographer shapes his image. Only after becoming somewhat familiar with the tradition of the iconographer can you gradually enter into his way of writing and painting. An icon is conceived in prayer and fasting and directed to liturgical service. It will only reveal its secret to a heart that is turned toward prayer and celebration—and even then, only up to a certain point.

The theme

It has been said that the first thing an iconographer writes is Tabor: the transfiguration of Jesus on a high mountain (see Mark 9:2-9; Matt 17:1-8; Luke 9:28-36). The meaning of the word *Tabor* was well known to the fathers of the church as well as to medieval authors. The Flemish mystic Ruysbroek, for example, in his short work entitled *The Sparkling Stone*, says that *Tabor* means "near to the light" (*tav* = near; *or* = light). According to

Icon of the Transfiguration
(Beginning of the Seventeenth Century, School of Novgorod)

the mystical literature of the Byzantine East, the light of Tabor is
in a class by itself. This understanding is especially found in the
works of the fourteenth-century writer Gregory Palamas. What
the gospels suggest is that the end of time is already to be seen
in the life of Jesus. The glory that is to come is shining out even

now, heralding what everyone is fervently hoping for (see Mark 8:38–9:1). In the gospel account only a few—actually, only three of those disciples who were the first to be called: Peter, James, and John—were worthy to see and bear witness to this light. The iconographer likewise must become worthy of the light, allowing himself to be completely penetrated by it so that, in spite of his limitations, it will shine forth and be received by those who venerate the icon he writes.

This particular icon provides an excellent résumé of all we have already seen and also opens our eyes to new horizons.

A vertical icon, whose center is emptiness

The first thing that strikes someone who gazes upon this icon is its vertical structure. The space is divided into three distinct sections: on the bottom, the three disciples; on the top, the Lord Jesus with Elijah and Moses; in the middle, an odd emptiness of desert and mountains. The three figures at the top occupy about half of the entire space. It seems that the icon was painted in such a way that it could be placed up high and seen from afar. As you continue to contemplate this icon your gaze is drawn upward, the mountainous midsection recedes into the background, and the whole composition seems to lean forward, with the three figures at the top appearing to come to meet you.

Another remarkable feature is that there is nothing in the icon to link the three figures on the bottom with those at the top. The middle section is completely empty, without any sign of a road or a path. There are only crevasses between the mountains, and they are all oriented in the same direction, from the bottom left to the upper right. In the same way the little rectangles of light, which seem to define the summits of the mountains, all move from the left to the right and from the bottom to the top.

I spent a good bit of time—six or seven years—trying to determine the meaning of the emptiness in the middle of the icon. At the very start I was convinced that the key to understanding the whole icon was to be found here. I could not accept the hypothesis that the iconographer had simply miscalculated, and that it would be a mistake to think that this empty space was of any importance. Such a hypothesis simply denied the problem and dispensed the viewer from going inside the icon in order to discover its meaning. We have to dwell in iconic space and become familiar with it, patiently awaiting the day when the significance of each tiny detail becomes clear and they all come together to reveal the meaning of the whole.

That is how it happened with me. One day the icon suddenly revealed its secret, like a ray of light that illuminates everything all at once. I can still remember the exact moment it happened. I was entering my room after having given an hour-long conference to the junior monks on the way of spiritual growth according to Evagrius, Cassian, and John of the Cross. Suddenly everything became clear. Ever since that day, my understanding of this icon has grown and the open space has continued to become larger and larger over the years.

The three disciples

Visually—and spiritually—everything seems to begin in the lower right-hand corner, near James. True to his name, he is upside down (see Gen 25:26!) and is shown in the position of a fetus in its mother's womb. A birth is about to take place; we all must become like little children. James holds one hand in front of his mouth, the other in front of his eyes: he does not yet have the gift of speech, and he is equally incapable of looking on the face of the essence of Light. Spirituality begins with this regression, this backward somersault, in which we remember our ultimate beginning. Is it not true that we must all be "reborn from on high," as Jesus said to Nicodemus?

The second figure appears to complement James perfectly. Instead of falling backwards, he is crawling forward on his hands and knees, although he still has to support his head, and his back is turned to the light. His position serves as a transition to the third disciple in the left-hand corner.

There we see Peter, who is getting back on his feet and gesturing like an orator. He is turned in the right direction and he speaks, doing what the first individual was totally incapable of doing: speaking and looking toward the true Light. He is the end point of the horizontal line that binds together the three figures at the bottom of the icon, and he is also the beginning of the line that moves upward. But he is still separated from the light, as far away from it as the other two. His words about the light do not bring him closer to it. As elsewhere in the gospel, here too Peter runs the risk of saying something that goes beyond his understanding ("He did not know what to say," Mark 9:6). He is like a pilgrim who goes on and on with stories about the road he has not yet traveled. The saying of Lao Tzu is especially apropos: "The one who speaks does not know. The one who knows does not speak."

The first stage of this icon depicts what might be called our horizontal development: from the condition of a fetus to the age of speech, from an existence that is still impersonal and unconscious to a life that is on its feet, responsible, and conscious of what remains to be done. As we grow in the spiritual life we cannot underestimate the importance of the first step, that of solid human formation. Spiritual freedom goes hand in hand with the exercise of mind and will. One can only begin the ascent of the mountain after the formation of an "ego" that is free and responsible, after having learned to identify and come to grips with the basic elements of one's own psychic life (law, the unconscious, the passions). In their descriptions of the spiritual journey, Evagrius and John Cassian connect this first stage with the active life (*pratikē*), which leads to purity of heart or the absence of passions and prepares one for the contemplative life (*theoretikē*).

The ascent of the mountain

The vertical movement unfolds in a way that is different from what we might expect. Right from the start we see the fundamental paradox: those who think they are winning are losing; those who are willing to abandon everything succeed; those who exalt themselves will be brought low; those who humble themselves will be glorified.

Peter now has to ascend this mountain. It is barren and there is no foothold. There is no trail, no greenery, no flower, no tree, no shade, no place to rest. Only crevasses and those strange little bursts of light on the ridges of the mountains. The iconographer points to the purification that is necessary if there is to be growth into a new and as yet unknown existence. There is no model to follow, no consolation on the way. Jesus suggests to Nicodemus the meaning of this new birth that we cannot even conceive of when he says metaphorically: "The wind blows where it chooses, and you hear the sound of it, but you do not know where it comes from or where it goes. So it is with everyone who is born of the Spirit" (John 3:8).

We must put aside our old habits of looking only at the surface of things and be willing to die to the senses and to what can be known through the senses. The way is one of total renunciation. What remains is created reality, rooted in the uncreated light, in the Word who was in the beginning. The soul that is thus purified takes delight in the face that glows in every creature, discerns the "logical" moment (to speak in a Greek manner) when the Logos, the Word, was one day joined to what was created. Through those little luminous surfaces on which everything seems to hang, the mountainous landscape evokes the hidden presence of the Word in every being. Only those who are pure in heart are able to see this mysterious divine presence shining like a light in all of reality. "In the beginning was the Word, and the Word was with God, and the Word was God. He was in the beginning with God. All things came into being through him, and without him not one thing came into being" (John 1:1-3). Evagrius and Maximus the Confessor say that contemplating the hidden bond between the original Wisdom and everything created belongs to this stage of the spiritual life, which is called "the first contemplation" or the *theoria physikē*.

Moses and Elijah

Those who do not turn away from this work of purification will eventually arrive at the place where Moses and Elijah are to be found. Both figures are impressive. They are slightly bent over, and there is a kind of hollowness at the core of their being, which is totally turned toward Christ. We need to look carefully at their physical posture; it has much to tell us.

The way they hold themselves is remarkable: their slight inclination shows them to be inwardly free and completely open, without the least resistance in the depth of their heart. Because they are empty within, they seem weightless, hardly touching the rock of the mountain. Their clothing catches the light of the one they contemplate and their very bodies appear buoyant and shining, like the body of someone who has fasted for a long time. Their hands tell us that they want to be intercessors, one by following his heart, the other by being faithful to the Word, the Torah. Both have entered into the heart of the great Secret, which is surrounded by a large black circle, the dark cloud. Moses seems to have gone a little farther into it than Elijah.

A new purification is here being brought to pass, a second "night" that is just as essential and productive as the first. The night is being ripped open by the rays of light that pass through it as they emerge from the cloud. Just as bursts of light shone on the ridges of the mountains in the region of the desert, here too ten rays of fire and light pass through the veil and begin to rip open the dark night. The two men of God are already in partial communion with this light that is so brilliantly and gloriously reflected on their clothing, hands, and faces. These glimmers of light and warmth are stronger than the obscurity and coldness of the dark night. At this stage of the journey they are the only signs given to believers to encourage them in their growth toward the One. Evagrius here speaks of the "second contemplation," which has the Trinity for its object and corresponds to "theology" in the proper sense of the term.

Jesus

To pass from Moses and Elijah to Jesus, the central figure, does not call for an ascent but a turning back, a final conversion. Upon entering into the cloud, what we find in front of us is our own most hidden and essential interiority. Here we discover something of the mysterious conversation St. Teresa of Avila recalls having had in one of the last dwellings of the interior castle. There she heard Jesus say to her, "From now on my concerns are your concerns, and your concerns are mine."

Jesus moves forward, upright and free. The real center of the large black circle is a radiant and gracious profile that is carried aloft by a powerful yet gentle force. His gestures are at once vigorous and serene. As he approaches, his bare feet show how vulnerable he is, but at the same time he appears invincible, as if nothing could stand in his way. He brings to mind the Suffering Servant of Isaiah 42: "he will bring forth justice," "a bruised reed he will not break," nor will he "be crushed" (vv. 1, 3, 4). With his right hand he gives a blessing, and in his left he holds a scroll—the Word that contains the will of the Father. The many pleats in his robe give evidence of the intensity of the life that fills him. No one can escape his gaze; it inspires fear, even though his entire person radiates kindness and humility. His own shoulders are perfectly relaxed, for he is carried by a power that comes from above and behind him. As this frail and gentle figure approaches us, the numerous geometric lines and the two concentric circles pierced by ten rays of light, all brilliantly colored, give off a commanding sense of presence.

Behind him a large vertical ray of light seems to be carrying him. Single in origin and triple in appearance, this ray says everything about the self-communication of the triune God. Jesus *is* this ray; he coincides with God's self-revelation: "Whoever has seen me has seen the Father" (John 14:9).

We are here in the presence of the "common man" (the "man of communion," *gemeyne mens*), described for us by Ruysbroek at the end point of the spiritual journey.[4] He is "common" and "familiar," close to us and "everything for everyone," just as

---

[4] See Paul Mommaers, *Wat is mystiek?* (Nijmegen: Gottmer, 1977), 84–93. See also Jan (van) Ruusbroec, *Ecrits I* ("La Pierre Brillante, Les Sept Clôtures, Les Sept degrés de l'amour, Livre des éclaircissements"), *Spiritualité Occidentale*, no. 1 (Abbaye de Bellefontaine, 1990), with the lexicon edited by Dom André Louf ("common," "communion").

God is, according to the vision of the Flemish mystic. As we see him here, he is strikingly near, free of all self-importance, and filled with an unguarded tenderness for everyone, small and great. This is the most human of all men, and yet he baffles us. His demeanor is entirely natural, but he is carried forward by an energy that is not of this world.

Breadth and width, height and depth, all dimensions are filled with light, glory, and the love that radiates from his disarming humility and power. Our contemplation of this Christ can never end, because what is evoked by this icon corresponds to the source of life that Jesus can make spring up in the heart of each disciple: "The water that I will give will become in them a spring of water gushing up to eternal life" (John 4:14).

A ladder of the spiritual life

Together the six figures form a single ladder bringing us to the knowledge and imitation of Jesus. The three classic stages of this movement are readily apparent.

The three figures at the bottom correspond to the first stage of the spiritual life as it has been understood in the monastic tradition since the time of Evagrius, namely, to the life of engaging in combat against the demonic forces. This stage involves a threefold dying to the old Adam: to the body (James), to one's character or psychic life (John), and to one's spirit or intellect (Peter). Dealing with these three levels of human existence is called the "practical" or "active" life and consists of the practice of virtue and the elimination of vice.

At the end of this first stage one arrives at what is called *apatheia*, the tranquility of spirit of one who has been freed of all unruly passions (Evagrius). John Cassian will rebaptize this term with an expression that is more biblical: the "purity of heart" (*puritas cordis*) that allows one to "see God" (see Matt 5:8). This purity coincides with what Cassian calls "the love of the Apostle," that is to say, the love extolled by Paul in 1 Corinthians 13, a love that is patient and kind, that "is not envious or boastful or arrogant," that "does not insist on its own way," "is not irritable," but "bears all things, believes all things, hopes all things, endures all things" (vv. 4, 5, 7).

Following this first stage comes the "contemplative" or "theoretical" life. According to Evagrius, it has two levels. At the first level those who are "pure of heart" contemplate the entire cosmos, everything that has been created, seeing it as anchored in God by the Logos. In our icon this first *theoria* or contemplation corresponds to the ascent of the mountain. Our purified vision now sees only the luminous face of things, their mysterious rootedness in the creative will and word of God.

At the final level the monk is invited to turn his mind exclusively to the mystery of the holy Trinity. Evagrius calls this the "second contemplation." In the icon of the transfiguration it corresponds to the movement by which Elijah and Moses enter into the dark night and give themselves over to the contemplation of God. Those who know the Son also know the Father, and this knowledge is bestowed on them by the Holy Spirit. "[N]o one knows the Father except the Son," and "no one knows the Son" except through the grace and good will of the Father, that is, in the Spirit (Mark 11:27).

Later Western traditions will also speak of three stages in the ascent to God. The terminology is only slightly different, and it has become well known in the West, thanks especially to Carmelite spirituality. These three ways are called *via purgativa* or the way of purification, *via illuminativa* or the way of illumination, and *via unitiva* or the way of union.

It is remarkable—but maybe not all that surprising—that this basic structure of the spiritual life, which was first spelled out systematically in the fourth century by Evagrius Pontus (d. 399), should appear in such a pure and readable form twelve centuries later in an icon from the north of Russia. I do not mean to suggest that the iconographer was consciously thinking of this tradition as he produced this work of art. But, as a writer of icons, he was part of a tradition, and by allowing us to read his own spiritual life in his work, he draws us into the spiritual space of a whole tradition.

We can thus see that there is another way of rediscovering Jesus, one that complements our study of the testimony of the first witnesses. Grounded in the traditions of exegesis, prayer, and spiritual practice, we prolong this scriptural tradition and invite others to come to know what is beyond all understanding: the mystery of Jesus, Jewish child and universal brother, son of a human being and icon of God. At the end of this journey we have traveled together, we are more disposed than ever to cry out with Paul, "I want to know Christ"! (Phil 3:10).

Come, Lord Jesus, come!
Lord Jesus Christ, Son of the living God, have mercy on me, a sinner.